creative
embellishing

creative embellishing

EASY TECHNIQUES AND OVER 25 GREAT PROJECTS

KAYTE TERRY

COLLINS & BROWN

First published in the United Kingdom in 2008 by
Collins & Brown
10 Southcombe Street
London
W14 0RA

An imprint of Anova Books Company Ltd

ISBN 978-1-84340-461-3

A CIP catalogue record for this book is available
from the British Library.

10 9 8 7 6 5 4 3 2 1

Reproduction by Rival Colour Management Ltd.
Printed and bound by CT Printing Ltd, China

This book can be ordered direct from the
publisher. Contact the marketing department,
but try your bookshop first.

www.anovabooks.com

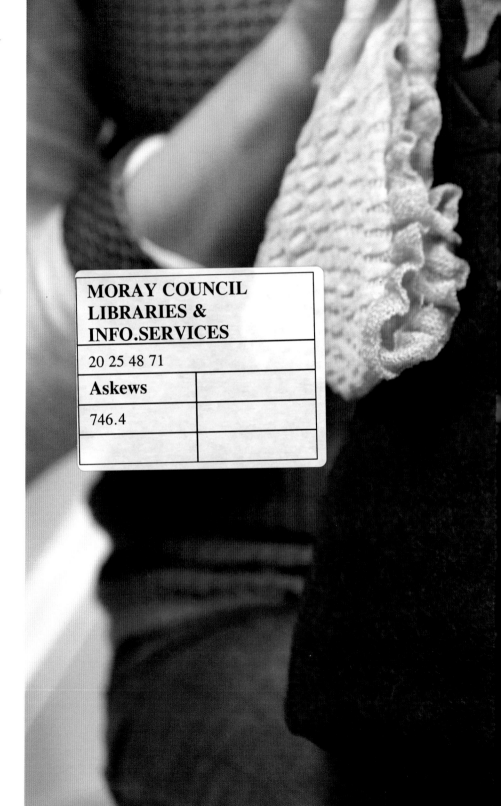

contents

introduction

I grew up in a craft-loving house. My mum was the ultimate do-it-yourself mother; our baby food was homemade; our clothes were hand-sewn; and as a child, my favourite toys were a set of wooden spoons, painted to resemble our family. When I wanted or needed something, my mum's first thought was not 'Where do I buy it?' but 'How do I make it?' Things were never thrown away; they were recycled and used for another purpose. I never really thought that I was missing anything then and now I know that I wasn't.

Don't get me wrong – I went through my rebellious phase. I practically lived at the shopping mall in 8th grade and all I wanted was to look like everyone else. Fitting in was paramount and my craft upbringing was not doing me any favours. Or was it? Looking back, I see things differently – my family couldn't afford the fashionable clothes I wanted, but thanks to my thrifty upbringing I knew I could find a lot of the same designer labels in secondhand shops. And all those fancy parties my friends invited me to? My mum made my dresses and no one ever knew. Just because you can make things doesn't mean you have to look like a hippy. Even if I was rejecting the DIY lifestyle on the outside, it was the only way I got through those tough middle-school years.

Flash forward quite a few years: I was living in Connecticut, working in New Jersey, and I was miserable. I hated where I lived; I hated my job; I didn't relate to any of my friends; and I had no creative energy. I sat in front of a computer all day aimlessly surfing the web, looking for something I could latch onto. One day, I found it. I had started getting back into crafting and I spent a lot of time looking for craft sites on the web. Most of them were not really my style, but I would take the techniques I learned and mould them into something that I thought was cool. One fateful day I stumbled on getcrafty.com and my life changed. I know what you're thinking – it's pretty sad that my life changed with a web site, right? Wrong – here was a web site devoted to cool, feminist women making crafts and, oh wow, here was this message board full of women talking about it, talking about everything – from making skirts and preserving vegetables to their jobs, boyfriends and girlfriends and everything in between. It was a revelation to find that there were people out there like me.

After a while, some of us decided we should meet. There were tons of ladies in New York City and I lived close enough to come in on the train. I was pleasantly surprised to find out that I liked these people offline as much as I had liked them online. Here was a strong group of women (and a few token guys) who really 'got' me. I am still friends with many of these people to this day: many of us are now pursuing crafts as full-time jobs; others prefer to make things for fun; but all of us are better for our love of crafts.

In the last few years, the craft movement has continued to grow stronger and gain more respect:

craft blogs are popping up everywhere; the Museum of Art and Design in New York recently held exhibits for artists who use crochet, lace-making and embroidery in a fine-art context; and when young tattooed hipsters on the subway pull out their knitting, no one even blinks. Once upon a time, you might tell someone at a party that you were into crafts and they would imagine their grandmothers at home making crocheted tissue-box covers (not that there's anything wrong with them – I love those things!) but today people actually have a reference point for craft and they know the myriad forms it takes. That's pretty cool. Crafting has come out of the proverbial closet and I couldn't be happier that more and more people are picking up knitting needles and embroidery hoops to make things themselves.

There is nothing more satisfying than making something with your own two hands. Of course it's easier to buy a new jumper at the store, but lots of people already have that same jumper. I love shopping and fashion as much as the next lady (actually, no, I love it a whole lot more) but I've learned that it's much more rewarding and fun (not to mention more economical and environmentally sound) to work with what I have. When I want a new jumper or a cooler bag, I just go through my wardrobe and try to reinvent something. Maybe that boring A-line skirt needs some frills or those jeans (that have been crumpled in a ball on the floor for months) would look better as a skirt. I love all of my clothes, but I am only truly proud of the items that I have made. By the way, this feeling extends to the way I decorate my home, too. Everything I own is open to embellishing!

Of course, in all my years of crafting, there have been some disasters too. There was the time that I tried to make a knit dress from a one-way stretch fabric and cut the fabric in the direction that doesn't stretch; or that really late night in college, when, fuelled by Diet Coke and junk food, I started hot-gluing buttons to my wall (the Facilities Department was not amused). But mistakes can be good too: you'll never make the same mistake twice, but more important, you may end up learning something that you never expected. Honestly, I have always been a bit of a messy learner and I can only really figure things out by digging in and trying it myself. Developing your craft side is really about developing your own creative processes. In other words, while there's often a wrong way to do something, there are many right ways.

I think it's time to stop talking and start crafting. I hope you enjoy making the projects in this book as much as I enjoyed dreaming them up. I encourage you to adapt them as much as you want or need. These are only starting points for your own creativity. Now go have some fun!

tools & techniques

This comprehensive section is full of useful techniques
and step-by-step photographs and illustrations that are
sure to set you on your way. Don't be afraid to expand
on any of the topics covered. Be creative and you
might impress yourself! From sewing and
embroidering to beading and fabric painting,
the myriad techniques included will allow you
to become a craft jack-of-all-trades.

embellishing basics

The first and most important part of embellishing is deciding what you would like to embellish. The possibilities are truly endless, so start looking around to see what you already have that can be improved, pressed back into service with a new use, or jazzed up a little just for fun!

Choosing Your Project

Look around. There are tons of boring old jumpers and faded T-shirts just begging to be reborn. Chances are, some of them are in your wardrobe already. Charity shops, car boot sales and secondhand stores are your next source. Think of all the items you see as works in progress. Tweed skirts look great with appliqués or bright ribbons and shapeless men's shirts can be totally transformed with a few pintucks.

In this first chapter, you will find all the information that you need about the basic tools and materials that are used for all the techniques and projects in this book. I have also covered all the basic techniques that I use for the projects in detail, with step-by-step instructions and either photographs or illustrations to illustrate each step.

The projects are divided into three sections: the first is garments; the second is accessories; and finally, items for the home are featured. Remember that you can mix and match ideas to your heart's content. An idea that I have used for a skirt could just as easily be adapted to make an embellished tablemat. Don't be afraid to experiment – if something doesn't work out exactly as you intended it doesn't matter. And you never know – it may turn out even better!

As is the nature of embellishing, your projects will probably look very different to mine – and so they should! Unless we shop at the same charity shops or frequent similar flea markets (and if that's true, stop following me!) your finds will certainly not be exactly the same as mine. The projects featured in this book are really intended to be starting points for you and your imagination. However, if you wish, you can follow exactly the designs, patterns and templates that I have created for this book. Or you can simply use the technique, or a mixture of techniques, to create your own totally original designs.

You may have a good local source of embellishing supplies, but at the back of this book you will find a list of resources that I use regularly to find my ribbons, trims, beads and fabrics. Most of these are either nationwide stores, or web sites from which you can purchase the items.

Happy Embellishing!

getting started

Make sure you read the list of materials and all of the instructions thoroughly before you start a project. Like baking a cake, crafting requires you to be prepared and have everything you need to get the job done. That doesn't that mean you shouldn't be creative – once you have learned some of the basic techniques, I would encourage you to find your own methods and shortcuts. I like to learn the 'right' way to do things before I go off on my own path and try out something new.

Your Embellishing Toolkit

For some projects you may need to buy special items, but tools and materials always to have on hand are:

Needles in different sizes: You'll want to have a variety of needles in different sizes for hand-sewing, embroidery, beading and many other uses. If you want to get really organised, keep them in a needle book by type.

Straight pins: You can buy these with glass, plastic or even flowered heads. I like to keep my pins in a pin cushion for accessibility.

Sewing and embroidery threads: It's also nice to have a good stash of basic colours in sewing and embroidery threads. When choosing a thread for a project, select one that is a shade darker than the dominant colour

in the project. You can usually get away with an all-purpose thread for most sewing projects, unless you are using very heavy or lightweight fabrics. I generally recommend avoiding cheap non-branded types of thread, because they break and fray very easily.

Water-soluble pen or tailor's chalk: These are great tools for marking lines or drawing designs on fabrics. Water-soluble pens work better on cottons and tailor's chalk is more appropriate for fabric with texture or those which water-soluble ink might bleed into. For marking straight lines, you can also use masking tape.

Fusible webbing: Fusible webbing takes the fuss out of appliqué. You can buy webbing in sheets, by the metre (yard), or in rolls. You only need rolls if you plan to do a lot of appliqué.

Fabric stabiliser: Fabric stabiliser stiffens fabric and also helps to keep it from moving around when you are embellishing it. You can purchase pin, iron-on or self-adhesive stabilisers, as well as stabilisers that tear away or dissolve in water. Stabiliser is essential when you are embellishing sheer or stretch fabrics.

Tracing paper: I use tracing paper for many different projects. It's useful when you want to alter an existing design or pattern. You can also trace patterns from this book and then alter them to fit your garment better. An 27.9 x 35.6cm (11 x 14in) pad of 25lb tracing paper is sufficient for most needs.

Lightweight cardboard: This is essential when making pattern pieces. It isn't necessary to purchase cardboard; I make patterns using cereal boxes.

Bias tape makers: Never buy packaged bias tape again! You can make your own bias tape quickly and easily with these little tools. Bias tape makers come in sizes that make 6mm (¼in), 12mm (½in), 18mm (¾in), 2.5cm (1in) and 5cm (2in) finished-width, double-fold bias tape.

Adhesives: Some of the adhesives I use regularly are fabric adhesive, jewellery adhesive, 5-minute epoxy and hot glue. There are tons of different adhesives out there, so just make sure that you are buying the right one to get the job done.

Fabric and paper scissors: All scissors are not created equal! You don't have to buy the most expensive fabric scissors, but purchase a good-quality pair and use them only to cut fabric. Paper scissors can be of lesser quality. To distinguish between the two, tie a small ribbon to the fabric scissors or mark them using a permanent marker. It is also nice to have small, sharp, pointed scissors for embroidery and for cutting threads. When I am working on a big project, I wear scissors around my neck on a ribbon so that I don't lose them amidst the piles of fabric.

Rotary cutter, straight edge and cutting mat:
A rotary cutter is indispensable for patchwork projects because you can accurately cut lots of identical pieces of fabric at the same time. Make sure you cut on a self-healing cutting mat. And use caution; rotary cutters are very sharp! I use a 45mm rotary cutter, a 90cm (36in) long straight edge and a 60 x 90cm (24 x 36in) cutting mat.

Embroidery hoop: An embroidery hoop keeps an area of fabric stable and taut while you are embroidering. Unless you want your embroidery project to be all puckered and bumpy, I would recommend using one. An 20cm (8in) diameter hoop will be ideal for most of your projects.

Planning Your Design

It is always a good idea to plan your design before you dig in. I think designing the project is always the most fun, so relish this process and take as much time as you need. A well-planned design leads to a beautifully embellished project. Advance planning also means that you will not be missing a vital element halfway through the work, or suddenly find that you haven't considered the next step and need to backtrack on work already done.

Advance planning

Here are some techniques I use to plan a design:

Never underestimate the value of a sketchpad. Sometimes inspiration strikes on the way to work or sitting on the tube, so I keep one with me at all times.

A digital camera is handy for referencing designs. You can lay out your design first and then look back at the record photo as you're working, to remember exactly where you pinned that flower or which colour sequin goes where.

Make a list of all the ingredients needed for a project, divided into items to purchase and items to gather. Put everything in one place and tick off the list before beginning.

sewing basics

Most embellishing projects will require some sewing, either by hand or by machine. Although you can use fusible webbing or fabric adhesive to apply a few types of decoration, sewing is the key for a more professional look and a durable finish.

Hand-Sewing

Hand-sewing is the foundation of most embellishing projects and many of the projects in this book can be completed easily without a machine. I find hand-sewing to be very relaxing and meditative. The best part is that you can take your project anywhere and work on it whenever you have a spare minute!

Running stitch

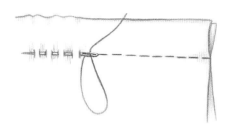

Slipstitch

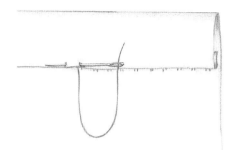

Hand-topstitching

Hand–sewing needles

Needles known as 'sharps' can be used for most hand-sewing. They are moderately long with a small eye. If you have trouble threading a needle, purchase a needle threader or use embroidery/crewel needles instead. They come in the same lengths and weights as sharps but they have larger, oval eyes. Use sizes 3 and 7. The higher the number in hand-sewing needles, the thinner and shorter the needle.

Machine-Sewing

Sewing machines may seem daunting to novice crafters, but don't be intimidated! Get to know your machine and you will love all the things it can do for you. Even the most basic machines will have several very useful functions.

Straight stitch **Small zigzag stitch**

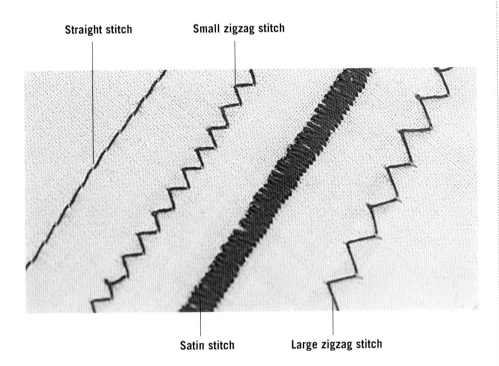

Satin stitch **Large zigzag stitch**

Machine-sewing tips

If you don't know your machine that well, read your manual. I consult mine to learn how to use a new function.

All the projects in this book have a 12mm (½in) seam allowance except where noted. The seam allowance is the area between the edge of the fabric and the stitching line.

The needle plate of your machine should have lines or marks showing different seam allowances. If it doesn't, measure sideways from the right of the needle and put a strip of masking tape on the needle plate to mark the seam allowance you want.

On a very curved seam, clip the seam allowance to within 3mm (⅛in) of the stitching before turning the project right side out. This stops weird bumps from forming in the seam. With a slight curve, trim the seam allowance to 5mm (³⁄₁₆in) and then clip.

Clip across a right-angle corner to within 3mm (⅛in) of the stitching to eliminate bulk.

Always use a sharp machine needle. A dull needle can cause missed stitches, especially on delicate fabrics.

Making Pockets

Adding extra elements to a garment is a great way to totally change the look. Follow these simple steps for great results every time.

1 Make a cardboard template of the pattern piece. Trace around template and cut out fabric piece, lining and interfacing.

2 Place lining right side up on interfacing. Place fabric piece right side down on lining. Pin all layers together.

Sewing-machine needles

Size 10 or 12 universal needles are fine for most sewing. For machine needles, the higher the number, the thicker the needle. If you constantly have trouble with threads shredding, use a needle designed for metallic thread. It has a larger eye and a larger scarf (or channel) in which the thread lies when the needle is inserted into the fabric.

Needles remain sharp for only six to eight hours of sewing and then must be replaced. It is a good rule of thumb to change your needle after every project.

3 Sew pieces together using 12mm (½in) seam allowance. Leave 7.5cm (3in) unsewn for turning (see Sewing tips, right). Trim seam allowance to within 5mm (³⁄₁₆in) of seam. Clip curves and across corners (see Machine-sewing tips on page 21).

4 Turn right side out, pushing corners out using a chopstick or other pointed tool. Fold raw edges of opening to inside and pin.

Sewing tips

When sewing an itcm that will be turned right side out, plan for an opening at least 7.5cm (3in) long. Start at least 12mm (½in) from a corner and on an uncurved portion of the edge. Always backstitch twice at the beginning and end of sewing so that the seam doesn't open when turning an item right side out.

Hand-topstitching is not only decorative, it keeps the edges neat so the piece stays nice and sharp. Omit this stitching if you want a less tailored look.

When working with large or complex pieces or with slippery fabrics, rather than pinning it's better to tack the layers together before sewing. Tacking holds the pieces more securely and sewing the item becomes less stressful for you.

5 Sew pinned opening closed using a whipstitch (shown here) or slipstitch (see Slipstitch on page 20).

6 You can either machine- or hand-topstitch 12mm (½in) in from all edges if desired.

Patchwork

I must confess that patchwork makes me dizzy with happiness. I love mixing patterns together, so patchwork is a natural match for my aesthetic sensibilities.

Quilter's ruler

If you think you may become a serious quilter, it's worth investing in a 90cm (36in) long quilter's ruler. They are transparent, usually 15cm (6in) wide and are marked in a grid, as well as with the various lines for the angles that you encounter most often when making quilts. The quilter's ruler is the best straight edge to use because its wider width holds fabric securely when rotary cutting.

1 To cut fabric for patchwork, you will need a rotary, straight edge and cutting mat. It's just so much easier and more precise than using scissors.

2 Use straight stitch and a 6mm (¼in) seam allowance to sew small pieces together first. Then sew the large pieces and complete the assembly.

3 Always iron seams, either all to one side (towards the darker fabric) or all open. There is a lot of debate as to which is the better method. I think it's up to the sewer, so find your preferred method and stick with it!

sculpting fabric

One of the basic techniques in embellishing is to add texture and to change the shape of the item with added sculptural features. Here's where yo yos, frills and pleats come in!

Yo yos

Yo yos are those cute little fabric puffs that look like rosettes. Though they were traditionally used for coverlets and have a country aesthetic, I think they can look quite modern and sculptural.

Tighten up

For a tightly gathered yo yo, use 6mm (¼in) long running stitches. For a more open centre in the yo yo, use running stitches that are 12mm (½in) long.

1 Cut a circle template twice the size of yo yo desired, adding a 6mm (¼in) hem allowance. Use template and water-soluble pen to draw a circle on wrong side of fabric. Cut out fabric circle.

2 Thread needle and knot thread end. With wrong side of fabric facing you, turn 2.5cm (1in) of hem to wrong side and fold under 6mm (¼in). Insert needle into hem on side facing you, 3mm (⅛in) from fold. Make running stitches around circle, turning hem under as you sew.

3 Pull thread to gather circle. Knot thread on inside hem. Centre gathers on yo yo and iron.

Frills

Frills are romantic embellishments to add to any project. They can be made from fabric, ribbon and other trims. You can use a gathering foot on your sewing machine or this low-tech method. Make sure that you account for the amount of fabric that you will need: for sheer fabrics, measure the length of the area to which you are applying the frill and multiply that measurement by three; with heavier fabrics, multiply the measurement by two.

Thread the needle and knot the thread end. Start close to one short end of the frill and make a running stitch 6mm (¼in) from a long edge. Make running stitches the length of the frill. End close to the other short end. Gently pull on the thread to gather the fabric to the desired length. Knot the thread ends to secure the frill.

It's easy and fast to gather using a sewing machine. Adjust the stitch to the longest length. Begin by backstitching twice. Sew along the long edge of the frill as for hand sewing. Do not backstitch at end. Cut thread ends to approximately 15cm (6in) long. Gently pull on the bobbin thread to gather the frill. Thread the bobbin thread into a needle and secure the frill by knotting thread.

Pleats

There are so many different kinds of pleats, it would take up a whole book to cover them all in detail! For our purposes, we are just going to learn how to make a basic pleat.

Pleats can be made as wide or as narrow as you would like, but be sure to measure accurately so they are even. For 12mm (½in) pleats, make a 12mm (½in) wide fold and pin. Continue by making 12mm (½in) folds every 2.5cm (1in) to the end of the length, pinning each fold. Hand- or machine-sew 6mm (¼in) from the pinned edge. Remove pins as you sew.

embroidery

Embroidery is a perfect way to add a little something special to a ho-hum garment or to highlight another embellishment such as an appliqué. Most of the projects in this book use cotton embroidery thread, but you can also try ribbons, perlé cotton, silk thread or yarn.

Basic Embroidery

Embroidery can seem tricky, but it's a lot easier when you use the right tools! Stabiliser works wonders when embroidering on knits or delicate fabrics. Dressmaker's paper makes it a snap to copy your designs onto fabric. There are hundreds of different decorative stitches you can use, but here are a just a few of the basic ones to get you started. Remember, always use an embroidery hoop.

Transferring skills

Copy design onto tracing paper or make a photocopy. Place tracing over fabric and slip dressmaker's paper, chalk side down, under tracing. Pin both to fabric to prevent them from shifting while you work. Working on a hard surface, go over all lines using a sharp, hard pencil. Check that the image has transferred by lifting up a corner of the tracing and dressmaker's paper.

Split stitch

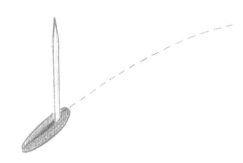

Blanket stitch

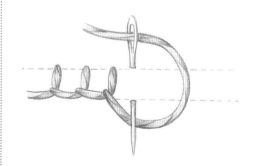

Backstitch

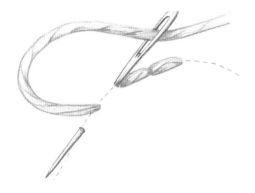

Satin stitch

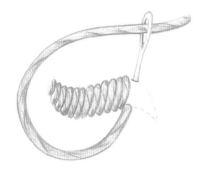

French knot

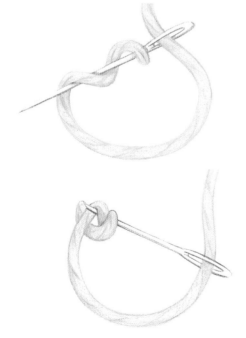

Chain stitch

Cross stitch

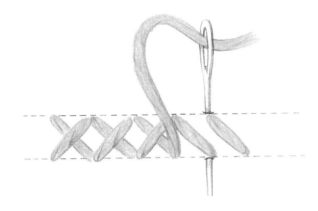

Lazy daisy stitch

Herringbone stitch

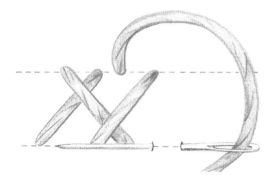

Feather stitch

Hoops and needles

Use a hoop large enough for the area. Fabric should be tight in the hoop and the fabric weave should not be distorted. Tighten tension adjustment if there is one.

The best needles for embroidery are called embroidery/crewel. They have a large oval hole and a sharp point. For embroidery, use three or more strands of thread and a size 7 needle. With fewer strands, use a size 8 needle.

Ribbon Embroidery

Ribbon embroidery has a romantic, old-fashioned feel that I really love. You can use many of the same stitches that you would for traditional embroidery, but the results will look different when using ribbon.

I use very narrow silk ribbons (2–4mm wide), which are available in a wide variety of colours. By twisting and looping the ribbons, you can also make realistic flowers (see Folded Ribbon Roses on page 36).

Spider web rose

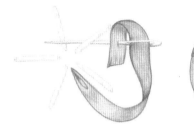

Running stitch

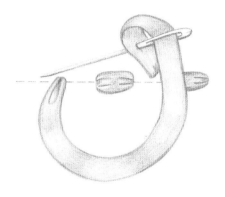

Ribbon stitch

Twisted ribbon stitch

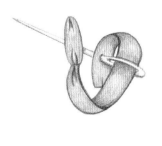

Basic couching

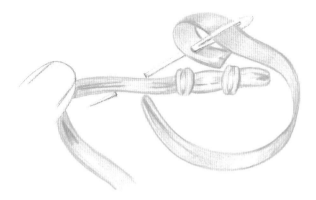

Fly stitch

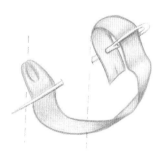

Gathered rosette

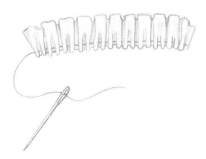

A stitch in time

Use chenille needles for ribbon embroidery. They have a large oval eye and a sharp point. For 2–4mm wide ribbons, use size 26; use size 24 for 7mm ribbon; and use size 18 for 13mm ribbon.

Needle size is important because the width of the needle's eye makes a hole in the fabric, allowing the ribbon to pass through without fraying. The fabric hole will be too small when using a size 26 needle with wide ribbon. Conversely, using a size 18 needle with narrow ribbon will make a large hole that can be seen once the stitch is completed.

It's difficult to keep a needle threaded with ribbon because the ribbon easily slips out of the needle's eye. To prevent this, a special technique is used for securing ribbon in the needle. Thread the ribbon end into the needle. Insert the needle tip into the ribbon 2.5cm (1in) from the end. Make a loose overhand knot close to the free ribbon end.

When ending, bring the ribbon to the wrong side of the work. Fasten the ribbon end on the wrong side using a hand-sewing needle and matching sewing thread.

Folded Ribbon Roses

Here's a very simple technique for making beautiful folded ribbon roses.

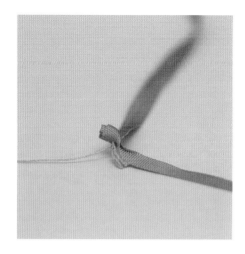

1 Thread hand-sewing needle with sewing thread to match colour of ribbon; knot end; and set aside. Cut a 30cm (12in) length of 4mm ribbon. Fold 2.5cm (1in) of one end of ribbon toward you on a 45-degree angle.

2 Roll diagonal fold onto longer end of ribbon five times to form centre of flower. Sew through bottom edges of flower centre to secure layers.

3 Fold longer end of ribbon away from you and on a 45-degree angle. Roll flower centre onto fold. Sew bottom edge to secure. Repeat by folding ribbon; rolling flower onto fold; and stitching. At the same time, roll the flower slightly higher each time to give depth to rose. Be sure to roll loosely. When flower is desired size, trim ends to 12mm (½in); tuck under rose; and tack to secure.

Using ribbon roses

Sew folded roses to your project by tacking the ribbon edges using matching sewing thread.

If you have the eyes and the patience, tiny folded roses can be formed from 2mm ribbon. The same technique can also be used to make roses from any ribbon width. Large roses made using 7.5cm (3in) wide, wire-edge ribbon make wonderful gift-wrap decorations or are a lovely addition to a wreath.

Duplicate Stitch

Duplicate stitch is an easy embroidery technique that mimics complicated intarsia knitting. Make sure that your item is knitted in stocking stitch (the knit looks like a series of Vs), or this technique won't work.

Plan ahead

To make a duplicate-stitch chart, copy a design onto graph paper. Each square on the graph paper equals one duplicate stitch.

Use a colour pencil to represent each yarn colour. Or, use a different symbol, such as +, –, x, or o, to represent each yarn colour. Make a key at the bottom of the graph paper, matching each symbol to a different yarn colour.

Determine where you want to locate the design on the knitted item. Mark the boundaries of the area using pins or tacking stitches. It may be easier to work all of the outside stitches first and then fill in. Or, work an entire area in one colour and then move to the next – it's your choice.

1 You will need an item knitted in stocking stitch; a size 16 tapestry needle; and a selection of contrasting colour yarns the same thickness and type as yarn in knitted item. Thread needle with yarn and knot.

2 Duplicate stitching is simply making V-shaped stitches over the existing V-shaped stitches on the knit. Bring needle from wrong side of knit to right side at bottom of a V.

3 Insert needle into top right end of V and exit at top left end of V. Insert needle back into bottom of same V to complete stitch.

crochet basics

If you don't have the patience for crocheting entire garments, then crocheted embellishments are for you! Crochet is a great craft because it's entirely portable and requires just a couple of tools – a crochet hook and yarn. Hooks come in many different sizes, starting with the diminutive 2.00mm (approx. B/1) – the smallest size – and going all the way up to a 'giant' 16mm (approx. Q). Here are a few basic crochet techniques to get you started.

Foundation Chain

The first step in crochet is the foundation chain, sometimes called the base chain, which is the basis for all crochet stitches.

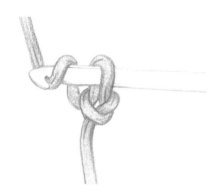

1 Make a slip knot by reeling off about a metre (yard) of yarn from the ball. Hold yarn in your palm 15cm (6in) from end. Using the yarn coming from ball, wrap yarn twice around your index and middle fingers. Pull strand coming from ball through loop between your two fingers, forming a new loop. Place this new loop on your hook. Tighten knot by pulling on free end of yarn. Adjust size of loop by pulling on yarn coming from ball until it fits hook.

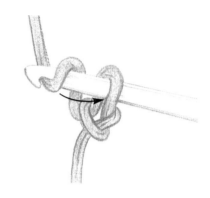

2 To make the first chain stitch (ch), wrap the yarn coming from the ball around the hook. This is called a yarn round hook (yrh) or sometimes yarn over hook (yoh).

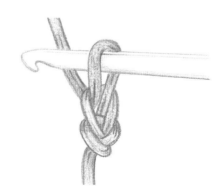

3 Use the hook to draw the yarn-over through the loop of the slip knot. You have made one chain stitch! Continue to yarn over and draw the yarn through the loop on the hook for each remaining chain stitch needed for your project.

Slip Stitch

A slip stitch (sl st) has many important uses, including making drawstring cords and joining the ends of a foundation chain to form a ring for crochet motifs worked in the round.

1 To make a drawstring cord, insert the crochet hook through both top loops of the first chain stitch from the hook. Yarn over the hook; then draw the yarn through the two top loops and the loop on the hook – one slip stitch has been made.

2 To join a foundation chain into a ring, insert the crochet hook through both top loops of the first chain stitch made. Yarn over the hook; then draw the yarn through the two top loops and the loop on the hook.

Fastening Off

After you have finished making your piece, cut off the remaining yarn, leaving an end of about 15cm (6in). Using the hook, pull this end through the last loop on the hook as if you were making a chain stitch, but pulling the end right through. Tighten the last loop to hold the end in place. If you want to use the end to sew up a seam, leave a much longer end before cutting off the excess yarn.

Blocking

It is essential to block your work if you want it to look its best. You will need a spray bottle filled with warm water, straight pins and a padded surface, such as a blocking board or padded ironing board. Form your crochet piece into the correct size and shape; then pin it down all around. Lightly mist over the entire piece with warm water until it is moist, but not soaked. Allow to air dry; then unpin.

Double Crochet

To work in double crochet (dc), the directions will ask you to crochet a foundation chain that has one more chain than the number of stitches needed for the project.

1 To make a double crochet stitch, insert the hook under the back loop of the second chain from the hook, then yarn over the crochet hook.

2 Now draw the yarn-over through the loop on the hook. You now have two loops on the crochet hook.

3 Yarn over the hook once more, then draw the yarn-over through the two loops on the hook.

4 You have made your first double crochet stitch. Continue to make a double crochet in each remaining stitch of the foundation chain. For next and each row that follows, chain one and turn. You will now be working through the two top loops of each double crochet stitch in the row below.

Half Treble Crochet

Io work in half treble crochet (htr), the directions will ask you to crochet a foundation chain that has two more chains than the number of stitches needed for the project.

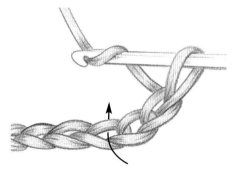 

Basic crochet abbreviations

beg: begin, beginning

ch: chain, chains

sl st: slip st

dc: double crochet

htr: half treble crochet

tr: treble crochet

dtr: double treble crochet

st/sts: stitch/stitches

t-ch: turning chain

yrh: yarn around hook

lp/lps: loop/loops

1 To make a half treble crochet stitch, yarn over the crochet hook, then insert the hook under the back loop of the third chain from the hook.

2 Yarn over hook, then draw the yarn-over through. You now have three loops on the hook. Yarn over hook, then draw through all three loops on the hook.

3 You have made your first half treble crochet stitch! Continue to make a half treble crochet in each remaining stitch of the foundation chain. For next and each row that follows, chain two and turn. You will now be working through the two top loops of each half treble crochet stitch in the row below.

Treble Crochet

To work in treble crochet (tr), the directions will ask you to crochet a foundation chain that has three more chains than the number of stitches needed for the project.

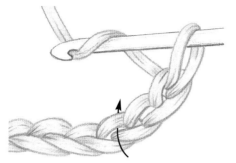

1 To make a treble crochet stitch, yarn over the crochet hook, then insert the hook under the back loop of the fourth chain from the hook.

2 Yarn over hook, then draw the yarn-over through. You now have three loops on the hook. Yarn over hook again, then draw through the first two loops on the hook.

3 You now have two loops on your hook. Yarn over hook once more, then draw the yarn-over through the last two loops on your hook.

4 You have made your first treble crochet stitch. Continue to make a treble crochet in each remaining stitch of the foundation chain. For next and each row that follows, chain three and turn. You will now be working through the two top loops of each treble crochet stitch in the row below.

Double Treble Crochet

To work in double treble crochet (dtr), the directions will ask you to crochet a foundation chain that has four more chains than the number of stitches needed for the project.

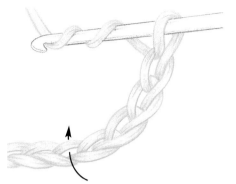

1 To make a double treble crochet stitch, yarn over the crochet hook twice; then insert the hook under the back loop of the fifth chain from the hook.

2 Yarn over hook, then draw the yarn-over through. You now have four loops on your hook. Yarn over hook, then draw through the first two loops on the hook.

3 You now have three loops on your hook. Yarn over hook, then draw through the next two loops on the hook. You now have two loops on your hook. Yarn over hook once more, then draw through last two loops on your hook.

4 You have made your first double treble crochet stitch. Continue to make a double treble crochet in each remaining stitch of the foundation chain. For next and each row that follows, chain four and turn. You'll now be working through the two top loops of each double treble crochet stitch in the row below.

trims and ribbons

Trims come in so many different types, shapes and sizes that it is just impossible to cover them all here. Basic trim types include bias tape, ribbons, rickrack, braid and lace.

Bias Tape

Bias-tape makers take the fuss out of creating your own custom tape and the makers come in the five most popular sizes of tape. Because the fabric used for bias tape is cut on the bias, the tape has a built-in stretch that easily curves around garment edges. Bias tape can be made from any fabric that holds a crease when ironed. It looks great sewn around a skirt hem or to finish the edge of a napkin. Because it's easy to shape into curves and curlicues, it also makes lovely design motifs.

1 Open fabric right side down on cutting mat, with selvedge (finished) edges at top and bottom. Fold top corner on a 45-degree angle until cut edge aligns with bottom selvedge edge. Finger press fold. Open fold, turn fabric right side up.

2 Use fold as a guide for first cut. Follow bias-tape maker instructions for fabric width needed. Cut strips using rotary cutter and straight edge. Cut one end of each fabric strip to a point. Insert fabric point into bias maker.

3 Press and pin fabric as it feeds through maker. To make double-folded bias tape, fold strip in half again and iron.

Ribbons, rickrack and lace

There is a trimming store in the garment district in New York that is my idea of heaven. Trims, lace and ribbons of all colours and sizes are displayed on shelves that reach the ceiling. On each visit, I find something that I have never seen before. Herein lies the appeal of trims: they aren't complicated to embellish with and there are so many available that you can customise each project according to your desires.

Ribbons and other trims

Making your own pleated trim

Trimming tips

Find the right trim for the job. Heavy ribbons such as velvet brocades and grosgrains have little flexibility so they can't be sewn around curves easily. Rickrack, bias tape and many laces are suitable for sewing around curves.

Pleat and frill ribbons and laces using the same techniques as for fabric.

Create your own trim by layering purchased trims. Sew narrow ribbons over a wider ribbon using decorative stitching for a trim that is unique!

felting techniques

When most people think of felt, they picture those synthetic squares that children use for craft projects, but wool felt is actually one of the oldest fabrics known. Wool felt is thick, tactile and gorgeous. You can make your own wool felt, or you can buy it by the yard. Felt can also be made from your hand-knitted or crocheted creations or by simply throwing a few old jumpers in the wash. You can also needle-felt using wool roving (thick yarn that hasn't been spun) or wool yarn to decorate garments or felted fabric.

Felting Jumpers and Other Wool Garments

If you have a jumper that doesn't fit or is full of holes and you want to sacrifice it to the craft gods, here's what to do. Just throw your wool garments into the washing machine with a small amount of detergent and wash on a medium hot cycle.

Felting tips

If you only need pieces of the garment, cut it up before you felt it.

Hot water felts better than cold water and putting the items in the tumble dryer will felt wool even more. The best felting occurs when the wool fibres are really agitated, so it helps to throw something, such as an old pair of tennis shoes or a tennis ball, into the wash to really get things going.

You can put items to be felted in the washing machine for a short cycle and take them out periodically to check on the felting process.

Once a garment is felted, it can be cut easily without the yarn unravelling.

Felting works best when 100% wool garments are used. Yarn blends with at least 60% wool will also felt, but the results aren't predictable.

Needle-Felting

You can needle-felt wool yarn, roving, or already felted fabric. You need a needle-felting tool (or single felting needles), needle-felting mat and the wool material onto which you want to felt. I like to use a needle-felting tool for felting flat designs and single needles for more dimensional work.

Making flat designs

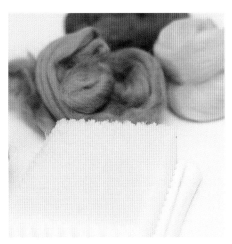

1 Set out your materials and tools. Decide on your design – let's say we will make a circle.

2 Take a small amount of roving; twist the ends slightly and coil to form a rough circle on the needle-felting mat.

Heartfelt

I prefer to make my shapes on the felting mat first. Then I place the area of the garment to be needle-felted face up on the felting mat and place the shape on it. I go over the entire shape again using the felting tool to secure, or felt, the shape firmly to the garment.

3 Use your felting tool to punch into the roving while at the same time carefully using your fingers to sculpt the shape.

Needle–felting tips

Dimensional designs can be needle-felted onto a garment with the single-felting needle. Working on the felting mat, punch the bottom portions of the design into the garment. Another method of securing the designs is to hand-sew them to the garment.

Cut-outs of previously felted fabric can be needle-felted onto a garment.

It's perfectly acceptable to needle-felt wool roving or yarn on a knitted garment that isn't 100% wool. In fact, the yarn needn't be 100% wool either, but yarn with a very high percentage of wool will work best.

Dry clean any garment that has been needle-felted even if it is washable. Needle-felting may loosen with the agitation and spinning of a washing-machine tub.

Making dimensional designs

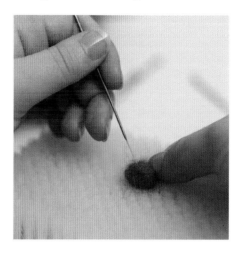

Roll a small amount of roving into a rough ball shape. Place ball onto the needle-felting mat. Use the single felting needle to shape it into a smooth ball, rolling and turning the ball as needed to felt it evenly.

Doing line work

Using a stencil

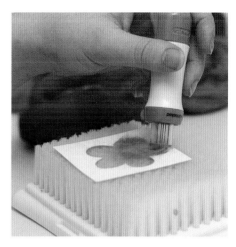

To make shapes, first cut a stencil out of cardboard. Then tape the stencil to the garment or tape it to the felting mat (if you wish to apply the shape to the garment after it has been needle-felted). Needle-felt, working up to the edges of the stencil.

You can also use yarn to draw lines or make letters. Pin the yarn onto the project and place it over the needle-felting mat. Punch the yarn with the felting tool, removing the pins as you work.

beads, baubles and sequins

For adding extra sparkle, nothing does the job like sequins and beads – and the best part is that you need only a few tools. To get started, you will need a water-soluble pen or tailor's chalk to mark your design on fabric. Most of the embellishment projects also require a needle and thread. If you are working on delicate or knit fabrics, you might want to add stabiliser to the back of the fabric and place the backed fabric in an embroidery hoop.

Beads

Beads can not only be used to add sparkle, but also to add colour and a three-dimensional element to your designs. You can either add beads one at a time, or stitch on several at once.

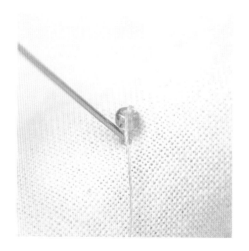

1 To sew on a single bead, insert needle from wrong side of fabric at point where you want bead to be secured. Thread bead onto needle and, with bead against fabric, insert needle into fabric on one side of bead.

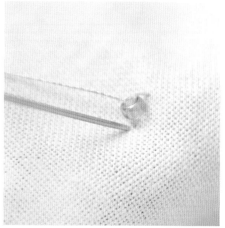

2 Bring needle through bead to right side of fabric. Insert needle into fabric on opposite side of bead. To add another bead, next to first, bring needle to right side of fabric, one-half bead width from first bead.

Adding multiple beads

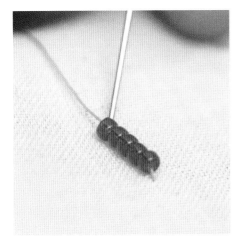  

1 To sew multiple beads at once, bring needle up from wrong side of fabric. Thread five beads onto needle and insert needle back down into fabric.

2 Bring needle back up through fabric between the second and third beads. Pass needle through third, fourth and fifth bead. Add next group of five beads.

3 Continue adding beads five at a time until design is complete.

Bead savvy

A size 12 beading needle works well for all but the tiniest seed beads.

Seed beads are the tiniest beads available and come in a number of sizes. Size 6/0 (the largest), 8/0 and 11/0 are the most popular sizes. Pony beads look like seed beads but are larger and range from 8 x 6mm to 9 x 7mm. Glass, crystal and gemstone beads can be round, in sizes 3mm, 4mm, 6mm, 8mm, 10mm, 12mm and 14mm. They also come in other shapes, such as oval, bicone, rondelle, cube, etc.

D-weight thread is compatible with most bead sizes. Some beading threads are available in colours. When sewing beads onto fabric, choose a colour that closely matches the fabric.

Buttons

While buttons often serve a utilitarian function, did you know that the first buttons to be used on clothing were purely for decoration? That's what we are going to be using them for in this book. If you don't want to sew on buttons, you can also glue them onto fabric or other materials using a permanent adhesive, such as jewellery adhesive.

Sewing a button

To sew on a button, thread a needle; double your thread; and make a knot at the end. Bring your thread from the back of the fabric and sew through the holes of your button, securing through all layers. Repeat three or four times.

Studs

Studs have sharp, pointed prongs on the back. These prongs are inserted through the fabric and then bent to secure the stud in place. It is important to do this properly to avoid any scratches or injury to your hands.

Shapes and sizes

The most popular sizes of studs are: 20 [5mm (³⁄₁₆in)], 30 [6mm (¼in)], 40 [9mm (⅜in)] and 60 [12mm (½in)].

There is a large range of stud shapes: round dome, round flat, faceted round, star, flower, heart – and many more. Studs come in metallic finishes such as gold, silver, gunmetal, antique brass and copper, as well as black, glitter and coloured enamel.

If you plan on using a lot of studs for projects, invest in a stud setter. This fairly inexpensive tool is easy to operate and will set sizes 20, 30 and 40 in much less time than doing it with pliers. It can also be used to set pronged rhinestones.

1 To set or secure studs, push prongs through fabric. Make sure all prongs push right through and fabric is smooth and unwrinkled.

2 Use needle-nose pliers to first bend prongs at a 90-degree angle to stud. Then curve point of each prong so it is inserted into fabric at centre of stud.

Sequins

Sequins are a great way to add individual points of light or a sparkly line to a project. Sequins come in a good range of shapes and sizes and can be either cupped or flat. Here are two ways to secure sequins.

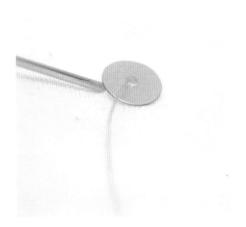

1 Thread needle and knot thread end. Bring needle from wrong side of fabric and through sequin. Make a stitch close to outside edge of sequin.

2 Bring needle from wrong side of fabric through sequin. Make a stitch, opposite first stitch, close to outside edge of sequin.

Using a bead

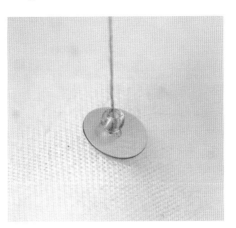

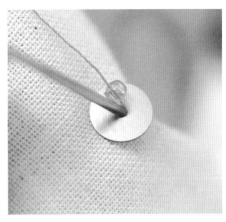

1 Bring needle from wrong side of fabric through sequin and bead.

2 Insert needle back into sequin and through fabric. The bead secures the sequin to the fabric. If it has a small hole, you will need to use a beading needle.

fabric printing

Printing images on fabric will add a whole new dimension and texture to both garments and home accessories. There are several different ways to accomplish this look, including stencils, image transfers, stamping and embossing.

Potato Printing

Potato prints are not just child's play. Using a potato stamp can yield modern, graphic prints that are perfect for fashion and home décor projects. The best thing about potato printing is it's an inexpensive technique.

1 Cut potato in half lengthwise and chill in the fridge for an hour. Blot up excess moisture using paper towel.

2 Use fine-tip permanent marker to draw design onto cut surface. Cut design with lino cutter, removing areas that should not print to about 3mm (⅛in) deep.

3 Use sponge to apply fabric ink evenly onto raised area of potato. Firmly press potato onto surface to be printed.

It's all in the fine print

When printing on fabric make sure you use a permanent fabric ink. Follow the manufacturer's directions to heat set the design with an iron.

Always allow the ink to dry thoroughly before heat setting.

To turn acrylic paint into permanent paint for fabric, combine it with fabric-painting medium, following all instructions on label.

Freezer-Paper Stencils

Freezer paper wasn't designed for stencils, but it's a great way to make stencils that will be used only a few times. Because it's inexpensive, you can try out lots of ideas.

1 Draw design on matte side of freezer paper, leaving at least 5cm (2in) border of paper on all sides. Cut out design on cutting mat using craft knife.

2 With shiny side of freezer paper face down, iron stencil onto right side of fabric using dry iron. Make sure stencil sticks completely.

3 Use small sponge brush to dab ink onto stencil. Don't brush on ink or it will run under edges of stencil.

4 Once entire design has been stencilled with ink, carefully peel off stencil.

Image Transfers

Ahh, the wonders of modern technology. Image transfers allow for the printing of computer-generated designs or photos onto fabric. There are many kinds of transfer papers for different types of applications. Be sure you read the manufacturer's directions to ensure your printer is compatible with the paper.

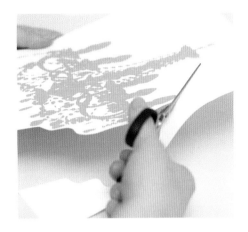

1 Print image on transfer paper. Cut out, leaving a 12mm (½in) border around all sides.

2 Place fabric, right side up, on a smooth, hard surface (not an ironing board). Position transfer, face down. Following the manufacturer's directions, iron the transfer.

Image makers

Because a transfer is placed on the fabric face down, any lettering in the design will be backwards on the fabric. To avoid this, make a flipped or reversed photocopy of the image and use that to print the transfer.

Transfers work best on fabrics with a smooth finish. Heavily woven fabrics, such as denim, can be used but the texture of the fabric may break up any fine lines in the design. For those types of fabric use bold designs with large, solid areas of colour.

3 Allow to cool; peel corner of transfer paper off carefully to check that image has been completely transferred. If it hasn't, go over area again with iron.

Dyeing Fabric

Each fabric dye is different and may require hot or cold water, as well as salt or other additives.

basic appliqué

Appliqué, from the French word 'appliquer', meaning 'to apply', is an ancient needlework technique in which one layer of fabric is sewn to another, usually a foundation fabric. Appliqué has come a long way since the invention of fusible webbing. You can use webbing to fuse fabric to a foundation fabric before stitching.

Getting started

With basic appliqué, fabric shapes in different colours are applied on top of a foundation fabric.

1 Place fabric right side down. Use an iron to fuse webbing, paper side up, to fabric.

2 Draw design on paper side of webbing and cut out shape. You can also trace design onto paper side of webbing before fusing it to fabric.

3 Remove paper backing and then use a warm iron to fuse shape to foundation fabric.

4 Embroider, using an embroidery hoop, or machine-sew around outline of design.

garments

Clothes are the most popular items for embellishing.
Everyone has a tired piece of clothing that they would
like to give a new lease of life. Or hunt through
jumble sales, secondhand stores, or local charity
shops for a likely item to embellish and make into
a star member of your wardrobe.

intermediate

★★

yo-yo yoke blouse

Yo yos often conjure up visions of vintage country quilts, but their shape can be sculptural and modern. I used yo yos on a silk blouse with a yoke for this project. If you have a strappy, sleeveless top that doesn't have a yoke, simply cut off the straps, sew yo yos together to make straps and then use yo yos to frame the neckline.

Materials

Pencil compass
Lightweight cardboard
Pencil
Ruler
Paper scissors
22.5cm (¼yd) each of
    three cotton prints
22.5cm (¼yd) of solid
    colour cotton
Water soluble pen
Fabric scissors
Sleeveless silk blouse
    with yoke
Straight pins
Hand-sewing needle
Matching sewing thread
Iron

1 Use pencil compass to draw four circle templates onto cardboard in the following four diameters: 6.5cm (2½in), 9cm (3½in), 12.5cm (5in) and 16.5cm (6½in). Cut out templates using paper scissors.

2 Use templates to trace several circles of each size onto each fabric. Cut out fabric circles using fabric scissors. Number of yo yos you need will depend on your blouse. I used 1 extra-large, 4 large, 14 medium and 16 small yo yos.

3 See Yo yos on page 26 for yo yo making technique.

4 Place extra large yo yo at centre bottom of front yoke. Pin yo yos on either side as shown. Make sure yo-yo yoke is symmetrical and covers blouse yoke completely. Pin yo yos to each other and unpin from blouse.

5 Use needle and thread to sew yo yos together on wrong side. Make sure stitching can't be seen on right side.

6 Pin yo-yo yoke to blouse. With wrong side of blouse face up, sew yo-yo yoke to blouse.

7 You can also add yo yos scattered over rest of blouse for a more organic look.

8 To retain their dimensional appearance, don't flatten yo yos when you iron blouse.

Ups and downs

For a subtle design, choose fabrics that match the colour of the blouse. For a more outrageous look, use contrast colours.

You can make yo yos lined in a contrast colour. Cut a second circle of fabric half the diameter and minus the seam allowance of the yo yo. Place the lining in the centre. Gather the yo yo with short stitches for a large centre opening, so the lining will be visible.

easy

★

vintage
appliqué dress

If you have ever spent any time at a flea market, you have probably noticed piles and piles of lovely embroidered vintage linens for sale. These linens are a powerful connection to our past and a reminder of the beauty people once crafted into their everyday possessions. Unfortunately, this also means that these linens often come with stains, along with the wear-and-tear of daily use. The Vintage Appliqué Dress is one way to re-use these well-worn treasures.

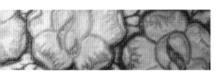

Materials

Assorted pieces of
   embroidered vintage
   linens
Iron
Wrap-over dress
   in cotton
Tape measure
Fabric scissors
Fabric adhesive
Hand-sewing needle
Matching sewing thread
Dress form (optional)
Seed beads in desired
   colours
Beading needle
Matching beading thread

1 Check your collection of
  embroidered linens and
make sure they're clean. Iron
them if they're wrinkled.

2 Measure edges of surplice
  neckline. Select an
interesting embroidery border
and cut two strips to length of
each neckline edge. Leave
about 6mm (¼in) of fabric on
either side of border. Dot back
of strips with fabric adhesive
and apply strips to neckline.

3 Find an embroidered motif
  that measures about 10cm
(4in) long by 7.5cm (3in) wide.
Cut out, leaving extra 6mm
(¼in) of fabric on all sides. Dot
back with fabric adhesive and
apply to dress right shoulder.

4 Find motif that is about
  22.5cm (9in) long by
12.5cm (5in) wide. Cut out,
leaving extra 6mm (¼in) fabric
around embroidery. Dot back
with fabric adhesive and apply
to right side of dress at
waistband, wrapping it slightly
around side of dress.

5 Try dress on to be sure that it's still comfortable and that you don't need to adjust position of any motifs.

6 Thread sewing needle and knot end. Secure neckline border and motifs to dress with running stitches (see Running stitch on page 20), sewing within 6mm (¼in) border. This step is easier if you have a dress form, although be careful not to stitch into it as you work.

7 Decide where you want seed-bead accents. I used red and yellow beads to accent flowers at waist, green beads for leaves at neckline and pink beads for bow at shoulder. You can add as many or as few beads as you like.

8 Thread beading needle with beading thread and knot end. Sew on seed beads (see Beads on page 50).

Quick fixes

I really like the shabby-chic effect embroidery motifs give when they begin to fray. If you prefer a cleaner look, you can apply a small amount of fray preventive liquid to the edges of each motif before you sew them to the dress.

Using the same technique but to achieve a slightly different look, cut out motifs from a fabric with a large floral print and machine-stitch them to the dress.

If you're really short on time, you could purchase premade embroidered motifs and sew them to your dress instead.

advanced

★★★

mod squad tee

Thrift addicts like myself often have a running list in our heads of things to look for when shopping. I have always been a sucker for shirts with giant collars and crazy prints. The problem is that they are usually made of synthetic fabric, which doesn't breathe at all. This embellished cotton T-shirt is a nice alternative. It has all the style of a vintage top but with a lot more comfort.

Materials

Paper scissors
22.5 cm (¼yd) of print
  fabric
22.5 cm (¼yd) of solid
  colour fabric
22.5 cm (¼yd) of
  lightweight interfacing
Straight pins
Fabric scissors
Sewing machine
Matching sewing thread
Iron
Scoop neck T-shirt in
  cotton
Hand-sewing needle
Tailor's chalk
Button-covering kit (if
  required)
Eight self-cover buttons,
  12mm (½in) diameter
56.5cm (⅝yd) of 12mm
  (½in) wide velvet ribbon
60cm (⅔yd) of 9mm (⅜in)
  wide velvet ribbon
Fabric adhesive

1 Enlarge collar pattern on page 169 to 225% or desired size. Cut out pattern using paper scissors.

2 Fold print fabric in half with wrong sides facing. Place pattern on fold and pin. Cut out using fabric scissors and remove pins. Repeat with solid fabric and interfacing.

3 Place solid fabric right side up on interfacing. Place print fabric right side down on solid fabric. Pin all layers together securely.

4 Pin collar to neck of T-shirt. Trim off any excess collar fabric along neckline. Unpin collar from T-shirt.

5 Machine-stitch around collar edges, leaving 7.5cm (3in) opening at centre back. Trim seams and clip corners (see Machine-sewing tips on page 21).

6 Turn collar right side out. Turn edges of opening to inside and pin closed. Hand-sew opening using slipstitch (see Slipstitch on page 20).

7 Machine-sew topstitching around collar 12mm (½in) from edge. Use tailor's chalk to mark centre back of collar.

8 Find centre front and centre back of T-shirt neckline and mark with tailor's chalk. Pin collar to neck edge of T-shirt. Match centre back of collar with centre back of neck on T-shirt.

9 Hand-sew collar to T-shirt using slipstitch.

10 Using button-covering kit (if required) and following manufacturer's directions, cover eight buttons with print fabric.

11 Cut two 11.5cm (4½in) lengths of 12mm (½in) wide ribbon for sleeve detail. Fold one end of each ribbon length under by 12mm (½in) and apply a tiny amount of fabric adhesive on wrong side to secure.

Mods and rockers

Feel free to experiment with different trims on this project: grosgrain ribbon, rickrack, or lengths of vintage lace would all look great.

Adding a collar is a great way to totally change the look of a top. You can even make several alternative collars in different fabrics and attach them with poppers instead of sewing them on. Then you can change the collar to match several different outfits.

12 Use tailor's chalk to mark edge of each sleeve at centre point opposite underarm seam. Pin ribbons to centre point (as shown in photograph on page 73) with turned-under top of ribbons 7.5cm (3in) from edge of sleeves. Turn other end of ribbons 2.5cm (1in) under sleeve edges.

13 Machine-stitch ribbons to sleeve, close to both edges of ribbon.

14 Hand-sew two covered buttons to ribbon on each sleeve, as shown in photograph on page 73.

15 Cut one 17.5cm (7in) length and two 10cm (4in) lengths of 12mm (½in) wide ribbon. Cut two 15cm (6in) lengths of 9mm (⅜in) wide ribbon.

16 Pin ribbons to front of T-shirt. For all ribbons, fold top 2.5cm (1in) end onto wrong side of T-shirt. Pin 17.5cm (7in) length to centre

Buttons

You can use purchased buttons instead of self-cover buttons on this tee. Choose washable buttons in colours that contrast or complement with the print fabric, depending on just how bold you want the effect to be.

front. Pin two 15cm (6in) lengths on either side of centre ribbon. Pin two 10cm (4in) lengths on either side of last ribbons pinned.

17 Machine-stitch ribbons to T-shirt, allowing some of the ribbon ends to hang free. Cut centre ribbon end into dovetail and cut others across at an angle.

18 Hand-sew remaining four covered buttons to centre ribbon.

intermediate

victoriana cardigan

Did you ever imagine your boring old cardigans had this kind of potential? This frilled and trimmed cardigan has been completely transformed with the help of felted jumper scraps from my felt stash. I love working with felted wool. The felting process shrinks the wool fibres so that no hemming is needed and felted wool stretches nicely so it is an easy fabric to use for embellishing.

Materials

V-neck cardigan in wool
Embroidery scissors
Tape measure
Rotary cutter, straight
    edge and cutting mat
Three felted jumpers or
    scraps from your felted-
    jumper stash
Sewing machine
Matching sewing thread
Hand-sewing needle
Straight pins
Dress form (optional)
Three sets of hook-and-
    eye fasteners
Needle-felting mat
Single needle-felting
    needle
Small amount of wool
    roving in two colours
Fabric scissors

1 Remove buttons from cardigan front using embroidery scissors.

2 With cardigan front facing you, measure front opening, from bottom edge on left side, around neck to bottom edge on right side.

3 Working on cutting mat using rotary cutter and straight edge, cut strips of felted jumper 6.5cm (2½in) wide (see Felting on page 46). For gathering, final strip must be twice the length measured in Step 2. Cut a sufficient number of strips and machine-sew together, using 12mm (½in) seams.

4 Thread sewing needle with thread cut to length in Step 2 plus 45cm (18in). Sew running stitches (see Running stitch on page 20) along one long edge strip. Pull thread to gather strip into a frill to the length measured in Step 2. Knot thread to hold gathers securely in place.

5 Align end of frill with inside bottom edge on left side of cardigan front. Cardigan edge should overlap gathered edge of frill by 12mm (½in). Pin frill around opening, ending at bottom edge of right side.

6 Machine-sew frill around edge of cardigan using straight stitch.

7 Add 5cm (2in) extra to measurement taken round front in Step 2.

8 Using rotary cutter and straight edge, cut 2.5cm (1in) wide strips of felted jumper. Cut and sew several strips together to make up length estimated in Step 7. I sewed two different coloured strips together for added interest, but you may choose to use just one colour.

9 Pin 2.5cm (1in) wide strip to right side of cardigan, turning end of strip 2.5cm (1in) to wrong side of cardigan. Have strip begin at bottom edge of left side. Pin around opening,

covering button holes and ending at bottom edge of right side. Turn end of strip to wrong side of cardigan.

10 Adjust sewing machine for a small zigzag stitch. Sew along both edges of strip.

11 Put cardigan on dress form, if available, or try it on. Use straight pins to mark three points where cardigan will fasten attractively. Hand-sew three hook-and-eye fasteners to cardigan where marked.

Making the flower

1 Roll a small amount of roving into a rough ball (see Making dimensional designs on page 48).

2 Place ball onto needle-felting mat. Use felting needle to shape into a neat ball, rolling and turning as needed to felt evenly. Make six balls, either in all same colour or in different colours. Set balls aside for the moment.

3 Using rotary cutter and straight edge, cut a strip of felted jumper 6.5cm (2½in) wide by 40cm (16in) long.

4 Use fabric scissors to cut scallop-shaped petals into one long edge of strip (see photograph, opposite).

5 Using rotary cutter and straight edge, cut a contrasting strip 5cm (2in) wide by 60cm (24in) long.

6 Cut scallop-shaped petals into one long edge of strip (see photograph, opposite).

7 Sew running stitches along uncut edge of each strip. Gather strips to about half their original length, when they start to curl.

8 Form 6.5cm (2½in) wide strip into a rosette and hand-sew all layers together at base. Repeat with 5cm (2in) strip. Place this on 6.5cm (2½in) strip and hand-sew both together.

9 Hand-sew felt balls to centre of flower.

10 Hand-sew flower to right side of cardigan.

advanced
★★★

layer cake t-shirt

Rows of frills and pleats always remind me of layer cakes because they are so deliciously feminine. This type of top always looks best when paired with your tightest jeans and boots, which add an edge to all that sugary sweetness. If your jersey fabric only stretches in one direction, make sure you cut it so the stretch runs across the T-shirt and not up and down, or you might have a hard time pulling the T-shirt over your head!

Materials

T-shirt (loose fitting)
Tailor's chalk
Tape measure
Paper
Pencil
45cm (½yd) each of
   two cotton jersey
   fabrics
Rotary cutter, straight
   edge and cutting mat
Sewing machine
Matching sewing thread
Straight pins
Fabric scissors
2.7m (3yds) of 2.5cm
   (1in) wide stretch lace
2.7m (3yds) of 6mm
   (¼in) wide elastic
Dress form (optional)
Hand-sewing needle

1 Put on T-shirt and use tailor's chalk to mark position of your waistline.

2 Measure 9cm (3½in) down T-shirt from first mark and mark again. Have a friend measure right around T-shirt at each mark, making sure tape measure is not pulled too tightly.

3 Multiply each of these measurements by 2 and add 5cm (2in) to each. Write measurements down, noting first one as 'waist' and second one as 'hips'.

4 Working on cutting mat and using rotary cutter and straight edge, cut strips from cotton jersey. For pleats at waist, cut one strip 4cm (1½in) wide and one strip 6.5cm (2½in) wide, to 'waist' length noted in Step 3.

5 For pleats at hips, cut one strip 4cm (1½in) wide, one 6.5cm (2½in) wide and one 10cm (4in) wide. All strips should be 'hips' length in Step 3. You may need to sew several strips together, using 12mm (½in) seam allowance, to get desired length.

6 Machine-sew 12mm (½in) long pleats every 2.5cm (1in) on all strips. If you want exact pleats, measure and pin strips before sewing (see Pleats on page 29). Or you can just estimate.

7 With right sides face up and sewn edges aligned, layer 4cm (1½in) waist pleat over 6.5cm (2½in) waist pleat and pin. Machine-sew together along stitching line.

8 With right sides face up and sewn edges aligned, layer 4cm (1½in) hip pleat over 6.5cm (2½in) hip pleat. Layer both over 10cm (4in) hip pleat and pin. Machine-sew together along stitching line.

Layers, layers, layers

For the ultimate in romance, skip the jersey fabric and pleat yards of stretch lace in different widths and colours.

Another cool option is to choose solid jersey fabrics in graduated shades. Start with the lightest as the first pleat and continue down the T-shirt with gradually darker coloured pleats.

9 Cut two pieces of lace without stretching it. Cut one to length of waist pleats and one to length of hip pleats. Pin lace to top of each pleated strip on right side. Have bottom edge of lace overlapping pleat stitching line by 6mm (¼in). Machine-sew close to bottom edge of lace.

10 Cut two pieces of elastic, without stretching it. Cut one to length of waist pleats and one to length of hip pleats. Pin to top of lace on wrong side. Machine-sew elastic to lace using widest, medium-length zigzag stitch.

11 If you have a dress form, place T-shirt on form. Pin pleats to chalk marks made in Steps 1 and 2. Overlap pleats by 2.5cm (1in) at centre back. Or, try on top and have a friend (carefully!) pin all pleats to T-shirt. Take care T-shirt is not pulled taut while it is being pinned.

12 Hand-sew pleats to T-shirt, removing pins as you stitch.

intermediate
★★

romance skirt

Every girl needs that perfect, swishy skirt that makes her feel like she's the star of one of those arty French films – this is that skirt. It's perfect for strolling along the Seine in the late afternoon or making your office party a little more chic.

Materials

90cm (1yd) fusible
 webbing
90cm (1yd) sheer fabric
 with a large floral print
Iron
Fabric scissors
Full skirt in taffeta
Pressing cloth
Sewing machine
Matching and contrasting
 sewing threads
Hand-sewing needle
Sequins in various colours

1 Peel off paper from one side of fusible webbing. Place sheer fabric over it, right side up. Iron fabric so that it adheres to webbing with no puckers.

2 Cut out several motifs in different sizes from fused fabric to make appliqués.

3 Peel off other side of paper backing from appliqués. Arrange appliqués on skirt as desired. Set your iron to a temperature that matches the fabric of your skirt and appliqués. Place a pressing cloth over appliqués when fusing, so fabric isn't damaged.

4 Machine-sew, using straight stitch and matching thread, along edge of all appliqués. For added interest, stitch in random patterns within appliqué shapes as well.

5 Using contrasting thread, sew around bottom of skirt in a random wavy, meandering line, running straight in a few places if you like. You can also sew around waistband if skirt has one.

6 Sew sequins to skirt in a random pattern of meandering lines (see Sequins on page 55).

Flower power

You could also cut out some of the larger motifs from a floral printed non-sheer fabric to make this skirt. Just make sure the fabric is light enough in weight so that the taffeta skirt can support all of the motifs.

An alternative idea is to use some small lace doilies or crochet motifs as your appliqué pieces.

easy
★

rainy day skirt

I got the idea for this skirt while I was rummaging through my local charity shop where plaid wool skirts abound. Appliqués are a quick and fun way to breathe new life into this old stand-by. I love mixing patterns with colours that complement the colours in the weave of the tweed. You can wear this skirt in any weather, but I guarantee it will brighten up a rainy day.

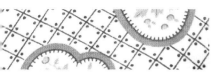

Materials

Black fine-tip permanent
  marker
Fusible webbing
Paper scissors
Fabric scraps in three
  different patterns
Fabric scissors
A-line skirt in plaid
Iron
Embroidery hoop
Size 7 embroidery/crewel
  needle
Embroidery thread in
  colours as desired
Embroidery scissors

1 Use marker to trace one
  small cloud and two large
clouds on page 173 onto paper
side of fusible web. Use a
photocopier to enlarge or
reduce clouds before tracing,
if desired.

2 Cut out clouds leaving
  2.5cm (1in) border on all
sides. Following manufacturer's
directions, fuse webbing to
wrong side of fabrics. Cut out
cloud appliqués (see Appliqué
on page 61).

3 Peel off paper backing and
  arrange appliqués on skirt.
Press each cloud with iron,
following manufacturer's
instructions.

4 Using four strands of
  thread in needle,
embroider split stitch (see Split
stitch on page 30) around each
cloud. Embroider over fabric
edge to prevent it from fraying.

5 Using six strands of thread
  in needle, embroider
running stitches (see Running
stitch on page 20) in various
colours below clouds to
indicate rain.

garden vine shrug

I learned how to needle-felt a year ago and I've been hooked ever since! It's such an easy way to transform dull jumpers into something beautiful. Once you get the technique down, you can adorn your wardrobe with any design your heart desires. Make sure your jumper is 100% wool or the design won't felt successfully! The petals and leaves on this shrug are felted separately, so secure them with small stitches on the reverse side.

Materials

Chalk-backed
    dressmaker's paper
Pencil
Shrug in 100% wool
Green, blue and purple
    wool roving
Small amounts of hot
    pink and yellow wool
    roving
Needle-felting tool
Needle-felting mat
Hand-sewing needle
Matching sewing thread

1 Enlarge design on page 170 to 125%. Make two copies, one reverse (or mirror image). You can alter design as needed to fit your garment, but make any changes before you transfer design to project.

2 Sandwich dressmaker's paper between photocopy of design and front of shrug. Go over all design lines using pencil to transfer design to shrug (see Transferring with chalk-backed dressmaker's paper on page 30).

3 To make vine, pull a long strand of green roving and roll it into a piece. Place on shrug following design line (see Needle-Felting on page 47).

4 Place felting mat under shrug and punch strand of roving using needle-felting tool. Continue punching, moving mat as you work, until vine is completed.

5 To make petals, pull a small piece of blue roving, twist it slightly and double it over into a petal shape. Place on mat and punch using needle-felting tool until petal shape is flat and roving is bound together.

6 To add purple detail, repeat technique in Step 5 using a slightly smaller piece of roving. Punch purple petal into blue petal. For each flower, make one large petal and two small petals.

7 Follow Step 5 and make leaves using green roving.

8 Place petals and leaves on shrug where indicated.

9 Place mat under shrug and punch each piece using needle-felting tool.

10 To make dots, roll small pieces of hot-pink and yellow roving into balls and punch them into shrug using needle-felting tool. Alter size of dots as desired to make an interesting design.

11 To further secure petals and leaves, use needle and thread to make small stitches on wrong side of shrug.

Green fingers

Don't have any wool roving? You can also cut pieces from wool felt scraps and needle-felt them onto the shrug.

If you are using a light-coloured garment, check that the roving or felt you are using is colourfast. You don't want your hard work ruined during your first handwash.

Even if you are doing a tiny detail, always place the area being felted on the felting mat. Never hold the work in your hands – felting needles are very sharp!

garden vine shrug   95

advanced
★★★

tulips and tweed jacket

Freezer paper was certainly not invented for making stencils – but it may as well have been because it is absolutely perfect for this technique! All you have to do is iron the freezer-paper stencil onto the garment you want to adorn and stencil away. This little tweed jacket looks great with a few strategically placed blooms in a shade of pink that really pops.

Materials

Chalk-backed
  dressmaker's paper
Pencil
Freezer paper
Cutting mat
Craft knife
Iron
Jacket in plaid
Small sponge brush
Fabric ink in pink or
  colour as desired
Pressing cloth
Assorted sequins
  (optional)
Hand-sewing needle
  (optional)
Matching sewing thread
  (optional)

1 Enlarge stencil designs on page 168 to 125%. Transfer or simply trace design onto matte side of freezer paper (see Transferring with chalk-backed dressmaker's paper on page 30).

2 Working on cutting mat, cut out stencils using craft knife (see Freezer-paper stencils on page 58).

3 With shiny side of freezer paper face down, iron large stencil onto right front of jacket. Make sure stencil adheres completely.

4 Dip sponge brush in ink and dab ink onto stencil. Don't brush on the ink or it will run under edges of stencil.

5 Carefully peel off stencil. Let stencilled design dry completely.

6 Repeat Steps 3–5 with small stencil on left front of jacket.

7 Following manufacturer's directions, heat-set designs with iron, covering design areas with press cloth.

8 If you choose, hand-sew some sequins to parts of design for a little added texture and sparkle (see Sequins on page 55).

Stencil style

To prevent jacket from shifting while you work, pin or tape it securely to your work surface.

If you are stencilling onto a lightweight fabric, such as a T-shirt, place a piece of cardboard between the front and the back of the garment to prevent the ink from bleeding through.

intermediate
★★

studded blouse

Think of this top as your 'first choice' for going out attire. The edginess of the hard metal studs is a perfect foil for the sensuous drape of the satin. Studs would look equally fabulous on a pencil skirt or a favourite pair of jeans. They are surprisingly easy to set and don't require expensive tools.

Materials

Satin blouse with
    waistband
Several packs of studs in
    different sizes, shapes
    and colours
Ruler
Water-soluble fabric pen
Needle-nose pliers

1 To determine how many
rows of studs you need for
your waistband, lay out studs
in one column. Measure and
then mark rows on inside of
blouse, using a water-soluble
fabric pen.

2 Working row by row, push
studs through blouse
fabric. Use needle-nose pliers
to bend prongs at a 90 degree
angle to stud (see Studs on
page 54).

3 Curve point of each prong
so that it is inserted into
fabric at centre of stud.

4 You may also choose to
add a few studs in a
random design to blouse ties.

Sparkle and shine

You can use studs to create a pattern on the bodice of the
blouse as well. Mark the pattern using water-soluble ink, then
apply the studs following your design.

This project would also look great if you substituted large
sequins or a selection of interesting buttons, instead of using
the studs. You could also try stitching on rows of crystals for a
subtle sparkle.

easy

vivienne vest

I love Argyle patterns, but sometimes they can be a bit, well, stuffy. With its frayed edges and yarn embroidery, this vest is more punk rock than prep school, à la Vivienne Westwood, one of my favourite designers. If you don't like vests, this pattern can easily be adapted to a skirt, a dress or even a tote bag.

Materials

Chalk-backed
   dressmaker's paper
Pencil
Lightweight cardboard
Paper scissors
Tailor's chalk
Old plaid skirt or 22.5cm
   (¼yd) tartan wool fabric
Vest knitted in wool or
   synthetic yarn
Fusible webbing
Iron
Sewing machine
Matching sewing thread
Worsted-weight yarn in
   three colours
Size 18 chenille needle

1 Enlarge diamond pattern on page 169 to 300% or desired size. Use dressmaker's paper to transfer diamond shape onto cardboard (see Transferring with chalk-backed dressmaker's paper on page 30). Cut out template.

2 Trace around template onto tartan, using tailor's chalk. Make sure fabric weave is parallel with diamond edges. Cut three diamonds; fray edges for 18mm (¾in) wide fringe.

3 Mark a line down centre of vest using tailor's chalk.

4 Cut fusible webbing for each diamond, remove paper from one side. Following manufacturer's directions, use iron to fuse webbing to wrong side of each diamond (see Appliqué on page 61).

5 Remove backing paper, place top diamond on vest approximately 5cm (2in) below neckline with points on chalk line. Use iron to fuse diamond to vest. Fuse middle and bottom diamonds to vest along chalk line, making sure points of diamonds touch slightly.

6 Using straight stitch, machine-sew diamonds to vest 18mm (¾in) from edges.

7 Referring to photograph, use chalk to draw lines for embroidered diamonds. Use running stitch (see Running stitch on page 20) and yarn to embroider fabric diamonds along stitching lines and chalk-marked diamonds.

intermediate
★★

daisy sundress

This little dress has comfy, roomy pockets perfect for holding sweets or just stashing necessities. You could embellish several dresses with different fabrics, one for every day of the week. You might not want to wear anything else!

Materials

Chalk backed
  dressmaker's paper
Pencil
Lightweight cardboard
Paper scissors
Water-soluble pen
22.5cm (¼yd) each of
  two cotton prints
22.5cm (¼yd) of solid
  colour cotton (for lining)
22.5cm (¼yd) of
  lightweight iron-on
  interfacing
Fabric scissors
Straight pins
Sewing machine
Matching sewing thread
Chopstick or other pointed
  tool
Simple dress or jumper in
  knit fabric
Seam ripper
Rotary cutter, straight
  edge and cutting mat
Iron
Dress form (optional)
Hand-sewing needle
Four buttons 2.5cm (1in)
  diameter

1 Enlarge pocket on page 169 to desired size. Use dressmaker's paper to transfer pocket onto cardboard (see Transferring with chalk-backed dressmaker's paper on page 30). Cut out template using paper scissors.

2 Use water-soluble pen to trace template twice each on one of the cotton prints, lining fabric and interfacing. Cut out all six pieces using fabric scissors.

3 For each pocket, press interfacing to wrong side of lining. With right sides facing, pin cotton print to lining.

4 Sew together using 12mm (½in) seam allowance. Leave 7.5cm (3in) unsewn for turning (see Sewing tips on page 23). Trim seam allowance to within 5mm (³⁄₁₆in) of seam. Clip curves and across corners (see Machine-sewing tips on page 21).

5 Turn right side out, pushing corners out with chopstick. Fold raw edges of opening to inside and pin.

6 Sew pinned opening closed using slipstitch (see Slipstitch on page 20) and iron.

7 Machine-topstitch 3mm (⅛in) in from edge on all sides, if desired. Set both pockets aside.

8 Use seam ripper to carefully remove straps from dress.

9 Measure straps. Multiply width by two and add 2.5cm (1in). Add 5cm (2in) to length.

10 Working on cutting mat, use rotary cutter and straight edge to cut two strips from second cotton print and two strips from interfacing. Iron interfacing to wrong side of cotton print.

11 For each strip, fold strip in half with wrong sides together and iron. Fold both long edges of strip 12mm (½in) to inside. Pin and iron.

12 Topstitch 3mm (⅛in) in from both edges of both straps.

13 If possible, place dress on dress form or place on flat surface. Pin straps to front and back of dress, in exact same locations as original straps.

14 Pin pockets to sides of dress, where desired.

15 Slipstitch (see Slipstitch on page 20) pockets and straps to dress.

16 Referring to photograph on page 109, sew buttons to dress.

advanced

★★★

ribbon
rose camisole

Ribbon embroidery is dainty, romantic and lends a wonderful dimensional quality to flowers that can't be achieved with traditional embroidery. These roses look perfect scattered across the top of a summery cotton tunic. Because it makes a pretty large impact, use ribbon embroidery sparingly, or you will begin to look like a wedding cake!

Materials

Chalk-backed
   dressmaker's paper
Pencil
Plain camisole in
   lightweight cotton
2.7m (3yds) 4mm-wide
   silk ribbon in each of
   peach, apricot, light
   green and medium
   green
Hand-sewing needle
Matching sewing thread
Straight pins (optional)
Tear-away stabiliser
   (optional)
Size 26 chenille needle
Embroidery hoop
Embroidery scissors

1 Enlarge pattern on page 170 to desired size. Transfer design to the front of camisole using dressmaker's paper (see Transferring with chalk-backed dressmaker's paper on page 30).

2 Thread a hand-sewing needle with sewing thread to match colour of ribbon, knot end and set aside. Make seven folded ribbon roses using apricot and peach ribbons.

3 For each rose, cut a 30cm (12in) length of ribbon. Fold 2.5cm (1in) of one end of ribbon toward you on a 45-degree angle (see Folded ribbon roses on page 36).

4 Roll diagonal fold onto longer end of ribbon five times to form centre of rose. Sew through bottom edges of rose centre to secure layers.

5 Fold longer end of ribbon away from you and on a 45-degree angle. Roll rose centre onto fold. Sew bottom edge to secure.

6 Repeat folding ribbon, rolling rose onto fold and stitching. At the same time, roll the rose slightly higher each time to give it depth. Be sure to roll loosely.

7 When rose is about 12mm (½in), trim ends to 12mm (½in); tuck under rose and tack to secure.

8 If camisole is made of very lightweight fabric, you may want to pin tear-away stabiliser to wrong side of fabric, behind embroidery, to reinforce the area and support the flowers.

9 Place camisole in embroidery hoop. Depending on the size of hoop, you may need to reposition it as you embroider leaves and stems.

10 Using medium-green ribbon, embroider stems by making lines of twisted ribbon stitches (see A stitch in time on page 34 for securing ribbon in needle, and Twisted ribbon stitch on page 33).

11 For all ribbon embroidery, fasten ribbon ends on wrong side of blouse with stitches, using hand-sewing needle and matching sewing thread.

12 Using light-green ribbon, work ribbon stitch for leaves (see Ribbon stitch on page 33).

13 Sew ribbon roses to yoke of tunic, making sure to hide all fixing stitching under flowers.

14 Tear away excess stabiliser on wrong side of fabric.

accessories

Even the simplest of outfits can become the height of
fashion when paired with the perfect accessory.
Keep up with trends or sport your own personal
style by giving your accessories a facelift using
these fresh embellishing techniques.

intermediate

patchwork pocket tote

Everyone needs a tote bag or two. This one's just great for groceries, library books or even a day at the beach. Patchwork may seem a little old-fashioned at first, but once you get the hang of making a patchwork square, you will find that the stylistic possibilities are endless.

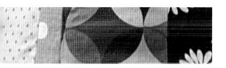

Materials

Plain canvas tote

Seam ripper

Tape measure

Rotary cutter, straight
   edge and cutting mat

22.5cm (¼yd) each of five
   cotton prints

Iron

Straight pins

Sewing machine

Matching and contrasting
   sewing threads

Fabric scissors

Water-soluble pen

22.5cm (¼yd) medium-
   weight iron-on
   interfacing

22.5cm (¼yd) solid cotton
   for lining

Chopstick or other
   pointed tool

Hand-sewing needle

Heavy-duty hand-sewing
   needle (size 7 sharps)

Embroidery scissors

1 Using a seam ripper, remove canvas straps from tote. Measure straps. Multiply width by two and add 2.5cm (1in). Add 5cm (2in) to length. Working on cutting mat, use rotary cutter and straight edge to cut two strips from two of the print fabrics.

2 For each strap, iron one long edge of strip 12mm (½in) to wrong side. Place canvas strap on wrong side of strip, with one long edge inside pressed edge of strip. Centre canvas strap from top to bottom of strip. Fold other long edge of strip over canvas strap, encasing it and iron. Turn long raw edge under, pin and iron.

3 Machine-topstitch both long edges 6mm (¼in) from edge, removing pins as you sew.

4 Work on cutting mat using rotary cutter and straight edge. From cotton prints, cut four pieces each in the following sizes:
A = 2.5 x 5cm (1 x 2in)
B = 2.5 x 10cm (1 x 4in)
C = 5 x 14cm (2 x 5½in)
D = 7.5 x 9cm (3 x 3½in)
E = 7.5 x 6.5cm (3 x 2½in)

5 Use 6mm (¼in) seam allowance to assemble blocks. Pin seams before sewing as needed. Iron seams as you work, pressing toward darkest fabric. Refer to block diagram below to assemble one block. Make four blocks.

6 Sew A to B. Sew A/B to C. Sew D to E. Sew D/E to C.

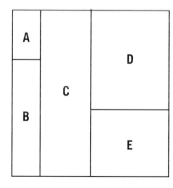

7 Sew four blocks together, arranging blocks to match photograph, or as desired. Iron seams.

8 Fold patchwork in half and use fabric scissors to trim one rounded corner through both thicknesses.

9 Using patchwork as template, trace same shape on interfacing and wrong side of lining fabric with water-soluble pen. Cut out pieces.

10 Iron interfacing on wrong side of lining. With right sides facing, pin patchwork to lining. Sew together using 12mm (½in) seam allowance. Leave 7.5cm (3in) unsewn for turning (see Sewing tips on page 23). Trim seam allowance to within 5mm (³⁄₁₆in) of seam. Clip curves and across corners (see Machine-sewing tips on page 21).

11 Turn right side out, pushing corners out with chopstick. Fold raw edges of opening to inside and pin. Sew opening closed, using slipstitch (see Slipstitch on page 20) and iron.

12 Pin pocket to centre outside on one side of tote. Slipstitch pocket to tote using hand-sewing needle.

13 Pin handles to inside of tote. Turn under ends 2.5cm (1in).

14 Thread size 3 needle with two strands of contrasting thread. To secure straps, sew 2.5cm (1in) square of stitching through all layers. Then sew an 'X' in the centre of each stitched square.

On the block

This tote has a patchwork pocket on only one side, but you could easily make pockets for both sides to double the carrying capacity!

The patchwork in this project is a simple design of asymmetric blocks, but you could use any quilt-block design for this project. Browse through a few quilting books to see if anything catches your eye.

If you only want a patchwork appliqué on your tote, omit the interfacing and lining and stitch your patchwork block to one side of the tote. Turn the edges of block 12mm (½in) to wrong side and iron. Pin; then hand-sew to outside of tote using slipstitch (see Slipstitch on page 20).

easy

★

bits and pieces scarf

A few years ago, I bought a gigantic box of doilies at a car boot sale (score!) and I have been incorporating them into many of my craft projects ever since. There are so many fantastic doilies out there, mostly made with immense care and attention to detail. Instead of tucking them into boxes and storing them in the attic, use them to make beautiful things that incorporate the vintage with the new!

Materials

Desired length of 25cm
(10in) wide tear-away
stabiliser
15 to 20 doilies in
different shapes and
sizes (Note: when
purchasing, lay out
your choices in shape
of scarf to make certain
you buy enough)
Digital camera (optional)
Paper (optional)
Pencil (optional)
Fabric dye in rose or
desired colour
Fabric dye in red or
desired colour
Large bucket
Protective gloves
Chopstick or paint stirrer
Paper towels (optional)
Straight pins
Sewing machine
Sewing thread in
matching or contrasting
colour, as desired

1 Place length of stabiliser on a large surface. Arrange doilies on stabiliser. Doilies should slightly overlap each other. If desired, use a rectangular doily at one end of scarf.

2 Take a photo of arrangement or make a simple sketch so that you have a record of the design to refer to when assembling.

3 Decide which doilies you want to dye. Dyed ones should be scattered randomly throughout the design.

4 Following manufacturer's directions, make rose dye bath in bucket. Wear protective gloves and cover your clothing and work area (see Dyeing fabric on page 60).

5 Wet doilies with clean water, then add to dye bath. Let them soak, following manufacturer's directions, stirring every few minutes using a chopstick or paint stirrer.

6 When you feel the colour is the shade you desire, rinse the doilies under cool running water until water runs clear. You can take the doilies out of the dye bath at slightly different times to get varying shades of colour.

7 Squeeze excess water from doilies, without wringing them, and gently pull them back into their original shape. Hang doilies to dry, or place them on paper towels.

8 Repeat Steps 4–7, using red dye and other doilies.

9 Referring to your record photograph or sketch, place dry doilies on length of stabiliser. Pin to stabiliser and to each other wherever the edges overlap.

10 Use medium-length straight stitch to machine-sew around each doily, removing any pins as you sew.

11 Tear away stabiliser from doilies.

Waste not, want not

When you are purchasing vintage doilies, it doesn't matter if they have a few light, minor stains because these will be concealed by the dye. If in doubt, wash the doilies before dyeing and use a prewash stain-removing product.

Avoid any doilies that are torn or have holes, unless you can work around them in your project. It's not easy to repair the lacy stitches unless you are an expert!

This project will be most successful if the doilies are made of threads of a similar weight, but don't worry about having lots of different designs. The more interesting the details, the better the effect!

Don't dye all the doilies. It's nice to leave a few of them in their natural vintage state to achieve that authentic shabby-chic look.

★★★

sakura blossom headband

A simple fabric headband becomes a confection fit for a fairy tale with the addition of crocheted flowers. I liked the idea that these flowers would dramatically frame the face, so I sewed some of them on the edge of the headband. If you are completely baffled by crochet (or just short on time), you can buy crocheted flowers at a haberdashery or vintage shop.

Materials

For the small flower:
1.8m (2yds) 4ply cotton
    yarn
3.25mm (D/3) crochet
    hook

For the medium flower and
layered flowers:
4.5m (5yds) DK weight
    cotton yarn in colour A
4.5m (5yds) DK weight
    cotton yarn in colour B
3.50mm (E/4) crochet
    hook
Size 16 tapestry needle

For blocking:
Straight pins
Blocking board or padded
    surface at least 6mm
    (¼in) thick
Spray bottle of water

For finishing:
Fabric-covered headband
Fabric scissors
Hand-sewing needle
Matching sewing thread

Small flower

1 Make a slip knot, leaving a
12.5cm (5in) tail and place
on crochet hook.

2 Ch4. Join ch with a sl st
forming a ring.

3 Round 1 (RS) *Ch4, sl st
into ring; repeat from *
around 4 more times more,
working over the tail
(5 ch-4 loops). Pull the tail to
close centre of flower. Thread
tail in tapestry needle; then
weave in tail on the wrong side.

4 Round 2 *In next ch-4
loop, work [sl st, ch2, 3tr,
ch2, sl st]; repeat from *
around 4 times more
(5 petals made). Cut yarn
leaving a 12.5cm (5in) tail.
Fasten off. Weave in tail on the
wrong side.

Medium solid colour flower

1 Make a slip knot, leaving a
12.5cm (5in) tail and place
on crochet hook.

2 Ch6. Join ch with a sl st,
forming a ring.

3 Round 1 (RS) *Ch4, dc in
ring; repeat from * around
4 times more working over the
tail. (5 ch 4 loops) Pull the tail
to close centre of flower.
Thread tail in tapestry needle;
then weave in tail on the
wrong side.

4 Round 2 *In next ch-4
loop work [dc, htr, 4tr, htr,
dc]; repeat from * around 4
times more (5 petals made).
Cut yarn leaving a 12.5cm
(5in) tail. Fasten off. Weave in
tail on the wrong side.

Two-colour layered flower

1 For top layer, use colour A
to make a slip knot, leaving
a 12.5cm (5in) tail and place
on crochet hook.

2 Ch4. Join ch with a sl st
forming a ring.

3 Round 1 (RS) *Ch4, sl st
in ring; repeat from *
around 4 times more working
over the tail (5 ch-4 loops). Pull
the tail to close centre of flower.
Thread tail in tapestry needle;
then weave in tail on the wrong
side.

4 Round 2 *In next ch-4
loop work [sl st, ch2, 3tr,
ch2, sl st]; repeat from *
around 4 times more
(5 petals made).

5 Working behind the petals
of the flower just made,
insert the hook through the
next space created by the ch-4
loop of Round 1 and dc over
the foundation ring; working in
the same manner, *ch 5, dc
into the foundation ring,

working through next space created by the ch-4 loop of round 1; repeat from * around 3 times more, ch5, join the round with a sl st in the first dc (5 ch-5 loops). Cut yarn leaving a 12.5cm (5in) tail. Fasten off. Weave in tail on the wrong side.

6 For bottom layer, join colour B with a sl st in any ch-5 loop of Step 5, in same ch-5 loop work [dc, htr, dc, 4dtr, tr, htr, dc], *in next ch-5 loop work [dc, htr, tr, 4dtr, tr, htr, dc]; repeat from * around 3 times more, join the round with a sl st in first dc (5 petals made). Cut yarn leaving a 12.5cm (5in) tail. Fasten off. Weave in tail on the wrong side.

7 Block the flower, as described above right, taking care to block the petals of each layer separately.

Blocking the flowers

1 Weave in all remaining loose tails on wrong side.

2 Place flower on blocking surface. Working one petal at a time, carefully stretch petal into shape and pin edges. Space pins no closer than 3mm (⅛in) and no further than 12mm (½in). Pin each petal until entire flower is pinned.

3 Pin all remaining flowers to blocking surface, spacing them about 2.5cm (1in) apart.

4 Use spray bottle filled with warm water to lightly mist each flower until slightly moist. Do not soak flowers.

5 Allow flowers to dry out thoroughly and then remove pins.

Sewing the flowers to the headband

1 Arrange the flowers on the headband and pin.

2 Use a needle with thread to match each flower. Working from wrong side of headband, tack each flower to headband.

Crochet abbreviations

ch = chain stitch
ch-sp = chain space
dc = double crochet
htr = half treble crochet
tr = treble crochet
dtr = double treble (triple) crochet
[] = Work the directions contained inside the parentheses into the stitch indicated.
sl st = slip stitch
* = repeat instructions following the single asterisk as directed.
RS = right side, right sides

On the block

You can use a well-padded ironing board or pad as a blocking board.

If flowers are just not your thing, you can find many patterns for a great variety of different crocheted motifs for your headband in crochet books.

easy

★

danish
blooms bag

Just because your bag is functional doesn't mean it has to be boring. I love the graphic, modern interpretations of botanicals that often find their way into Scandinavian designs. They always look beautiful against a rich wool fabric. Remember, this design is not about perfect circles but rather the beauty in the shapes of flowers.

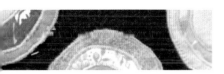

Materials

Scraps of wool felt in
   shades of blue and
   green
Scraps of cotton prints
Fabric scissors
Straight pins
45cm (½yd) of 25cm
   (10in) wide tear-away
   stabiliser
Sewing machine
Matching or contrasting
   sewing thread as
   desired
Fabric adhesive
Solid-colour tote bag in
   wool

1 Each flower is made of three circles. You will need three circles in each size. From contrasting shades of felt, cut 10cm (4in) diameter and 5cm (2in) diameter circles. From print fabric cut 7.5cm (3in) diameter circles. The circles needn't be perfect; that's part of the charm of this design.

2 Cut three straight stems and six leaves from green felt, using the photograph (left) as a guide.

3 Cut two vines with leaves from green felt. Cut vines a little shorter than length of bag straps.

4 For each flower, pin large circle to a slightly larger piece of stabiliser. Machine sew around circle using satin stitch or buttonhole stitch. Centre medium circle on large circle and sew in the same way. Repeat for small circle. Tear away stabiliser from assembled flowers.

Blooming marvellous

For a different look, use a more traditional floral design, but be sure the shapes are simple and stylised.

If you prefer, stitch the flowers using satin stitch in a contrasting rather than a matching thread colour.

5 If desired, pin each leaf, stem and vine to a piece of stabiliser and machine-sew around as in Step 4. Tear away stabiliser.

6 Use fabric adhesive to glue felt pieces to bag.

intermediate

pearl
button purse

For a subtle take on evening sparkle, pearl buttons are a nice change from the usual sequins. I buy jars of buttons at flea markets so that I have lots of them lying around for a project such as this. If you want speedy results, you could decorate this bag without taking out the lining, but a new lining will make it more special.

Materials

Fabric clutch purse

Embroidery scissors

Large selection of pearl
   buttons in assorted
   shapes and sizes

Hand-sewing needle

Sewing thread in light
   pink, or as desired,
   to sew buttons

Seam ripper

30cm (⅓yd) cotton print
   for lining

Straight pins

Fabric scissors

Sewing machine

Sewing thread to match
   lining

1 Cut lining from purse using embroidery scissors. Do this neatly, leaving a 12mm (½in) border of lining attached to inside. Set lining aside.

2 Using shape of purse as a guide, arrange buttons in an attractive design on your work surface. I have arranged mine in a random pattern, with a cluster of buttons at the frame and then spacing them gradually farther apart toward bottom of purse.

3 Have a doubled-strand of thread in needle. Begin and end sewing on inside of purse. For each button, begin with knotted thread and end by knotting thread on inside. Start sewing at frame, with buttons slightly overlapping as in shown in photograph.

4 Use seam ripper to separate lining removed in Step 1 into two pieces. Use one piece as pattern. Fold lining fabric in half, matching short edges. Pin lining piece to

fabric. Cut out, adding 2.5cm (1in) to top edge. Machine-stitch side and bottom seams same as original lining. Fold top edge 12mm (½in) to wrong side and finger press. Place lining in purse. Pin folded edge to border of original lining, about 6mm (¼in) from frame. Hand-sew lining to border using slipstitch (see Slipstitch on page 20).

Pearly whites

If the vintage pearl buttons you purchase are a bit grimy, give them a good wash before you use them. Put a tiny amount of liquid soap in a jar with some warm water. Put in the buttons and shake the jar well to agitate everything. If there is any stubborn dirt left on any of the buttons, just use a soft brush to scrub it away.

If you prefer a bit more sparkle on your purse, you could use this same design but stitch on either various shaped sequins or a selection of crystal beads.

easy

★

quick shoe embellishments

Shoes may seem like they would be difficult to embellish, but a quick trip to the haberdashery proves otherwise. You can adorn all your shoes with pretty trims, charms or beads, customising them to reflect your many stylish whims. I personally like the designs on my shoes to face me (otherwise it just looks weird when I look down at my feet) but it's really up to you. Here are a few ideas.

Materials

Fabric scissors
Ruler
Hand-sewing needle
Matching sewing thread
Jewellery adhesive

Baroque shoe trims

60cm (⅔yd) of 1mm
  (⅛in) wide green velvet
  ribbon
6.5cm (2½in) long oval
  cameos
Pair of gold leather flats

Punky shoe trims

30cm (⅓yd) of 4cm
  (1½in) wide red tartan
  ribbon
30cm (⅓yd) of 21mm
  (⅞in) wide blue tartan
  ribbon
Two kilt pins in gold
Straight pins
Size 12 beading needle
Beading thread in white
  or transparent
Twenty-four 6mm pearls
Pair of yellow canvas
  flats

Baroque shoe trims

1 Cut ribbon into two 30cm (12in) lengths. Thread needle and knot end. For each ribbon, sew running stitches 3mm (⅛in) from one long edge (see Running stitch on page 20). Gather ribbon to about half its length (see Frills on page 29). Turn ends under and form into an oval. Test the fit of cameo on oval and either tighten or loosen gathers. Knot thread to hold gathers.

2 Protect work surface from glue drips. Fold ends of gathered ribbon to wrong side and glue.

3 Apply jewellery adhesive to gathered edge of ribbon, keeping the oval shape. Glue cameo to centre of ribbon oval. Be careful not to get excess glue on ribbon.

4 Determine which way you want cameos to face – they can either face you or face the world. Referring to photograph on previous page, glue ribbon oval to shoe.

Punky shoe trims

1 Cut each length of ribbon in half. Trim ribbons so that they are unequal lengths. Cut all ribbon ends into dovetails as shown.

2 Fold each ribbon roughly in half. Fan ends out, then layer blue tartan on top of red plaid and pin close to fold. Hand sew ribbons together close to fold.

3 Protect work surface from glue drips. Apply jewellery adhesive along non-opening edge of kilt pin. Refer to photograph – clasp of one kilt pin should face left and other face right. Fold sewn edge of ribbon assembly over glue to secure. Let dry.

4 For one shoe: thread beading needle and double-knot end. Add dot of glue to knot. String on five pearls. With clasp of kilt pin facing left, align fourth pearl on ribbon fold, to left of ribbon edge. Insert needle into ribbon fold and exit at left of fourth pearl. Pull thread tight. Pass needle back through fourth and fifth pearls. Make small stitches at back of ribbon fold to secure. First three pearls strung at left will hang free.

5 String three pearls on needle. Skip last pearl strung and pass needle through second and first pearl. Make a stitch into ribbon fold and pull thread tight. Make small stitches at back of ribbon fold to secure.

6 String four pearls on needle. Skip last pearl strung and pass needle through third, second and first pearl. Make a stitch into ribbon fold and pull thread tight. Make small stitches and knot at back of ribbon fold to secure. Trim thread close to knot. Dot knot with glue.

7 For other shoe. follow Steps 4–6, changing 'left' to 'right'.

8 Open kilt pins and secure to top of shoes, making sure clasps will face away from each other on pair.

intermediate

ultraviolet scarf

Duplicate stitching mimics the look of intarsia knitting, but the technique is actually based on embroidery. For this project, I was inspired by the colourful screen-printed flowers of Andy Warhol and so I named the scarf after one of his Factory regulars.

Materials

Graph paper (optional)
Pencil
Highlighter
Scarf knitted in stocking
    stitch
3 colours of yarn in same
    weight and yarn as
    scarf
Size 16 tapestry needle
Embroidery scissors

1 In the chart on page 171, each square represents one duplicate stitch. This design has three flowers on one end of scarf and one flower on other end. You can alter size of flowers, if needed, by making your own chart on graph paper (See Duplicate stitch on knits on page 37).

2 Thread needle with yarn and knot end. A duplicate stitch is an embroidered V-shaped stitch covering a V-shaped stitch on knitted item. Bring needle from wrong side of knit to right side at bottom of a V. Insert needle into top right end of V and exit at top left end of V. Insert needle back into bottom of same V to complete stitch. To end a strand of yarn, make a few tiny stitches on the back. Cut off yarn end quite close to stitches.

3 Follow chart to embroider design. Cross off completed rows using pencil or highlighter so you won't lose your place in the chart.

Pattern tip
It's easy to create your own duplicate stitch chart using graph paper and a set of coloured pencils.

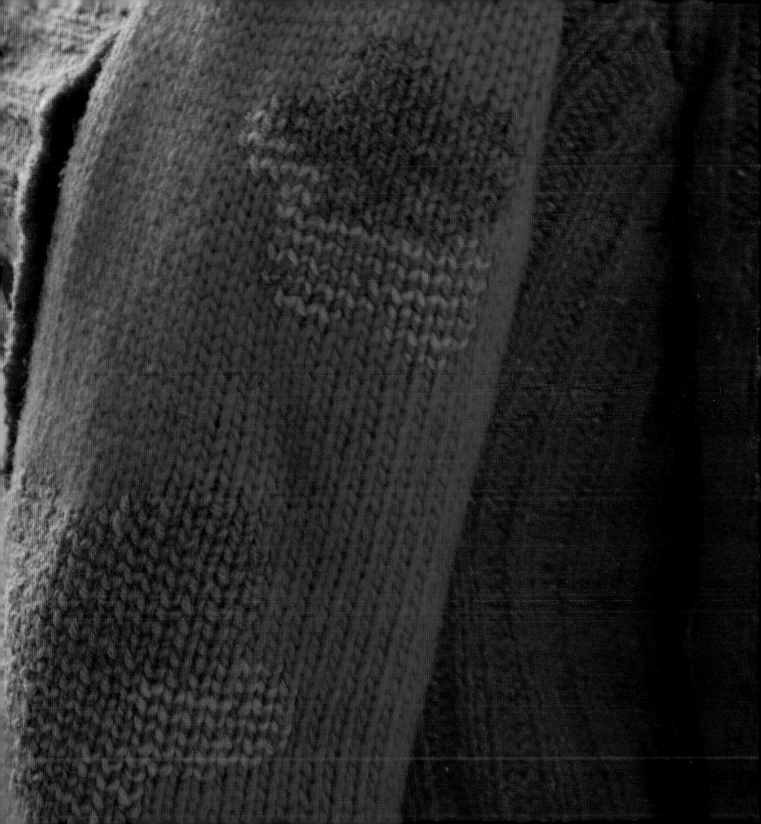

home furnishings

Don't limit yourself to clothing and accessories when embellishing. You might be surprised to find a wealth of furnishings crying out for that little extra something around your home. Recycle vintage fabrics, add embroidery to plain napkins to make them suitable for a special dinner party or brighten up your kitchen with painted tea towels.

trompe l'oeil lampshade

Chandeliers are the ultimate in design sophistication, but are often pricey and would be a big hassle to install in a rented flat. This modern and easy-to-make lampshade would look stunning hanging from the ceiling over a single light bulb or on a large floor lamp. The chandelier images appear to be complex stencils, but they are really just image transfers printed on an ink-jet printer.

Materials

Colour ink-jet copier/
   scanner/printer
Four to five sheets iron-on
   image transfer paper
   (Note: quantity depends
   on size of lampshade)
Paper scissors
Iron
22.5cm (¼yd) white cotton
   fabric
Fabric scissors
Newspaper
Spray adhesive
33cm (13in) diameter, or
   larger, drum lampshade
   in white
Embroidery thread in
   desired colours
Size 7 embroidery/crewel
   needle
Embroidery scissors
20 chandelier drops in
   crystal or acrylic
Satin-finish spray paint in
   desired colour
Tape measure
Ice pick
Needle-nose pliers
20 gold 8mm jump rings

1 Scan chandeliers on pages 172 and 173, enlarging them as desired (see image transfers on page 59).

2 Following manufacturer's directions, print four to five chandelier images onto image transfer sheets.

3 Cut out, leaving 12mm (½in) border on all sides.

4 Place fabric right side up on smooth, hard surface (not an ironing board). Position transfer, face side down. Following manufacturer's directions, iron the transfer.

5 When transfer is cooled, peel off transfer paper carefully. Check that image has been completely transferred. If it hasn't, go over area again with iron.

Lights out

For more elaborate embellishment, embroider on the image transfer after transferring it to the fabric and before adhering it to the shade. Use some of the decorative embroidery stitches shown on pages 30–32, working them in thread colours that will reflect the overall décor of your room.

6 Cut around chandelier images, leaving 12mm (½in) border of fabric around all sides.

7 Place chandelier images, face down, on newspaper and apply spray adhesive.

8 Stick chandelier images to lampshade as desired, referring to photograph.

9 Thread needle with three strands of embroidery thread and knot end.

10 Use running stitch (see Running stitch on page 20) to sew chandelier images to lampshade.

11 In well-ventilated area (outside if possible), place chandelier drops on newspaper and apply an even coat of spray paint. Allow to dry, turn over and then spray other side.

12 Measure circumference of bottom of shade. For a 33cm (13in) diameter shade, the circumference is slightly more than 100cm (40in). For spacing of chandelier drops, divide the circumference by 20. For this size lampshade, spacing is slightly less than 5cm (2in). Use ice pick to lightly pierce shade 20 times just above bottom wire. The holes are for jump rings, so keep them small.

13 For each crystal drop, use needle-nose pliers to open a jump ring. Slip drop onto jump ring. Insert one end of open jump ring into hole in shade, then use pliers to close jump ring.

easy
★

folk art
tea towels

Some people may think potato-printing is for children, but the process is perfect for creating graphic Scandinavian-style designs. I also love the idea that I can run to the corner shop to pick up my printmaking supplies. Make sure to buy yourself a big bag of potatoes to experiment with because potato printing is addictive.

Materials

Tracing paper
Pencil
Chalk-backed
  dressmaker's paper
Lightweight cardboard
Paper scissors
Potatoes
Sharp knife
Paper towel
Fine-tip permanent
  marker in black
Lino cutting tools
Cotton or linen tea towels
Fabric ink in two different
  shades of orange,
  yellow, turquoise and
  green
12mm (½in) sponge
  brush
Ruler
Iron

Making a stamp

1 Trace motifs on pages 168 and 169. Use dressmaker's paper to transfer all motifs onto pieces of cardboard (see Transferring with chalk-backed dressmaker's paper on page 30). Cut out template.

You say potato...

You can use your potato stamps again. They will keep in the refrigerator for a day or so, but after that, throw them away.

If you want to print one colour over another, allow the first to dry completely, or colours may run together. This could be an interesting effect, but experiment on scrap fabric first.

For best results, make sure the ink is applied evenly to the stamp. This will ensure nice, sharp prints. Reapply colour as soon as the print begins to break up.

2 Cut potatoes in half lengthwise using knife. Blot excess moisture with paper towel (see Potato printing on page 56).

3 Use marker to trace template onto cut side of a potato.

4 Use lino cutting tools to cut around outline of template, then remove all areas that should not print. Lino cutting tools are very sharp so always cut away from yourself. Put finished potato stamp into refrigerator for at least an hour before printing.

Stamping a motif and heat setting

1 Place towel on work surface. Brush fabric ink onto stamp. Use even pressure to stamp onto towel.

2 Allow ink to dry out thoroughly. Heat-set fabric ink with an iron following manufacturer's directions.

Seed pod tea towel

1 Cut one large and one small seed-pod stamp.

2 Use two different orange inks to stamp pods in both sizes all over towel.

Flower-stalk tea towel

1 Cut one stamp each for flower centre, petal, stalk and leaf.

2 Use yellow ink and stamp flower centre in centre of towel width and about 5cm (2in) from end of towel.

3 Stamp a turquoise petal on either side of flower centre as in photograph.

4 Stamp green stalks down centre of towel.

5 Stamp green leaves next to stalks as shown.

framed inspiration board and button pins

Forget those generic corkboards. To get your creative juices flowing, you are going to need a really beautiful inspiration board. I use mine to tack up postcards, tear sheets from magazines, old photos and anything else that inspires creativity. Adorable button pins make the board even more fun to use.

Materials

For the inspiration board:

Picture frame in desired
size
Medium- and fine-grade
sandpapers
Damp cloth
Acrylic paint in desired
colour
2.5cm (1in) wide paintbrush
Water-based varnish
5mm (³⁄₁₆in) thick foam
board cut to fit frame
Print fabric cut 5cm (2in)
larger on all sides
than foam board
Hot-glue gun
Glue sticks
Twelve 3cm (1¼in) wire
brads
Tack hammer
Ruler and pencil
Awl or ice pick
Two 4cm (1½in) long
sawtooth hangers with nails

For the button pins:
Drawing pins
Assorted buttons
Heavy-duty wire cutter
Jewellery adhesive

1 Sand frame, first with medium-grade sandpaper and then with fine-grit sandpaper. Wipe sanding dust off using tack cloth.

2 Paint frame following manufacturer's directions. Apply two to three coats, as needed. Allow each coat to dry for two hours.

3 Apply two coats of varnish. Allow each coat to dry for two hours.

4 Place fabric, right side down, on work surface. Centre foam board on fabric.

5 Apply line of hot glue on one long edge, 2.5cm (1in) from edge, and at both corners. Immediately fold fabric over edge of foam board and smooth it onto hot glue. Repeat for other long edge, this time pulling fabric so it is smooth and tight on front of foam board. Hot glue is hot, so be careful to protect your fingers.

6 Repeat Step 5 for short edges of foam board.

7 At each corner, fold fabric neatly and stick down with hot glue.

8 Place covered board in frame. Use wire brads hammered into back of frame to secure board. Use at least three wire brads on each side.

9 On back of frame, measure and mark 7cm (2¾in) from each corner of frame top.

10 Measure and mark 18mm (¾in) from top of frame to each mark made in Step 9.

11 Position each sawtooth hanger centred on mark made in Step 9. Place top edge of hanger at mark made in Step 10.

12 Use awl to make pilot holes for nails. Secure hangers with nails.

Making the button pins

1 If there is a sewing shank at back of button, clip it off using wire cutters.

2 Apply small amount of jewellery adhesive to top of drawing pin and back of button. Stick drawing pin to button and allow to dry.

Mix it up

Another design option for button pins is to layer buttons and glue them together before sticking to the drawing pin. Adding a small brass charm to the top button is a nice touch.

Don't feel that you have to use identical buttons for your pins. Using a variety of sizes, colours and designs will make your board even more exciting and different.

advanced
★★★

collector's napkins

I love to look at beautifully displayed collections of natural objects. These napkins were inspired by display cases filled with exotic insects. Due to the nature of embroidery, each insect will look a little different and each of your collector's napkins will be one-of-a kind. These napkins would be a special wedding gift for a couple too cool for monograms!

Materials

Chalk-backed
    dressmaker's paper
Cotton or linen dinner
    napkins
Straight pins
Pencil
Embroidery hoop
Embroidery thread in
    colours as desired
Size 7 embroidery/crewel
    needle
Embroidery scissors
Towel
Iron

1 Enlarge motifs on page 170
to desired size.

2 Place photocopy over
corner of napkin and slip
dressmaker's paper, chalk side
down, under photocopy. Pin
both to fabric to prevent
shifting while you work.

3 Working on a hard
surface, go over lines with
a sharp, hard pencil. Check
image by lifting up a corner of
photocopy and dressmaker's
paper (see Transferring with
chalk-backed dressmaker's
paper on page 30).

4 Place design area on
napkin into embroidery
hoop (see Embroidery on
page 30).

5 Thread needle with three
strands of thread for all
stitches. To begin and end
work with a strand of thread,
make tiny stitches on wrong
side of napkin.

6 Use backstitch for details
and outlines. Fill larger
areas with satin stitch. Other
decorative stitches can be used
as desired. (See stitch
illustrations on pages 30 to 32.)

7 Place embroidery, right
side down, on folded towel
and iron gently to remove any
wrinkles.

Bug bear?
Not a fan of bugs? Look
through copyright-free
books of motifs published
by Dover Books for more
inspiration.

These designs would look
great on clothing or fabric
accessories. I like the idea
of them on crisp
pillowcases.

You can also draw your
own designs and transfer
them onto the napkins.

intermediate
★★

woollen
bunny

This little bunny is inspired by my very own real-life muse, Potato. I started making little bunnies out of jumper scraps to give to my friends shortly after my husband and I adopted Potato. He spends days with me in my craft room 'helping' me sort fabric, chewing on my papers and hopping all over my projects. I couldn't live without him.

Materials

Lightweight cardboard
Chalk-backed
 dressmaker's paper
Pencil
Paper scissors
Water-soluble pen
Felted jumper (for bunny
 body)
Assortment of felted
 jumper scraps (for
 details)
Straight pins
Fabric scissors
Size 7 embroidery/crewel
 needle
Embroidery thread in
 desired colours
Embroidery scissors
Two buttons, matching or
 in different colours
 as desired
Sewing machine
Sewing thread to match
Fibrefill stuffing
Chopstick or other
 pointed tool
Hand-sewing needle

1 Enlarge bunny on page 1/1 to desired size. Use dressmaker's paper to transfer bunny onto cardboard and cut out template. (See Transferring with chalk-baked dressmaker's paper on page 30.)

2 Pin template to jumper. Use water-soluble pen to trace bunny template onto wrong side of jumper. Cut out from both thicknesses. Cut details from scraps; pin to right side of bunny.

3 Use three strands of thread in needle and knot end. Sew details to bunny using whipstitch (see photograph of whipstitch on page 23). Embroider nose using backstitch and satin stitch. Sew on buttons for eyes.

4 With right sides facing, pin front to back. Use straight stitch to machine-sew 12mm (½in) from edge. Leave 7.5cm (3in) opening in one side.

5 Clip corners and curves. Turn right side out, using chopstick to push out ends.

6 Stuff small pieces of stuffing tightly into all parts of bunny body with chopstick.

7 Turn edges of opening to inside and pin opening closed. Hand-sew opening closed using slipstitch.

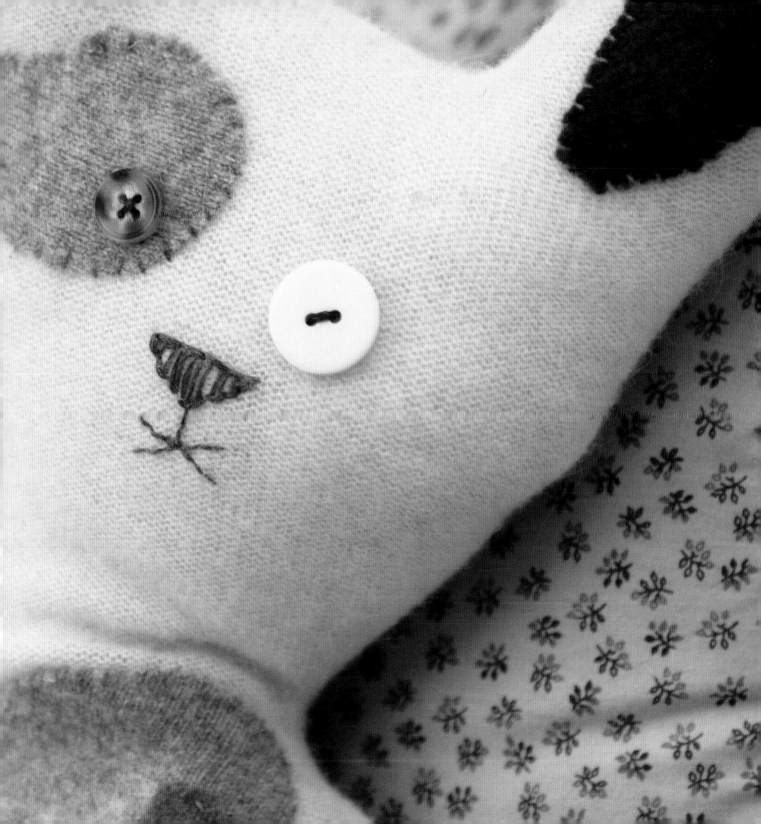

**Tulips and Tweed
Jacket, page 96**

Folk Art Tea Towels, page 152

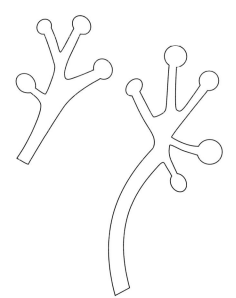

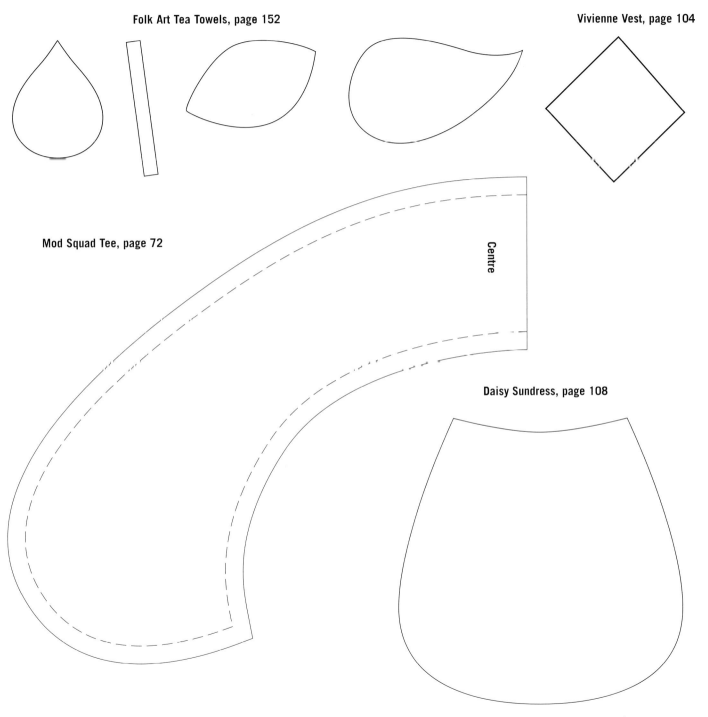

Folk Art Tea Towels, page 152

Vivienne Vest, page 104

Mod Squad Tee, page 72

Centre

Daisy Sundress, page 108

Ribbon Rose Camisole, page 112   **Garden Vine Shrug, page 92**   **Collector's Napkins, page 160**

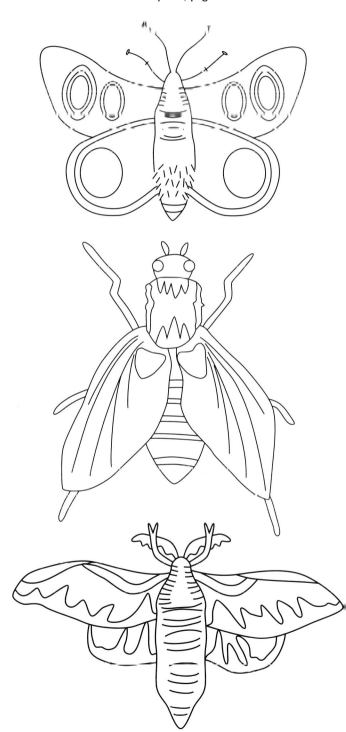

Ultraviolet Scarf, page 142

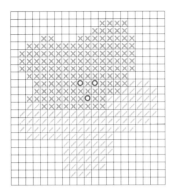

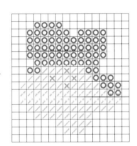

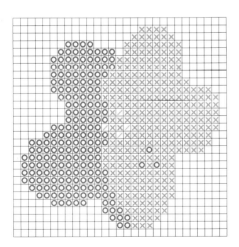

Woollen Bunny, page 164

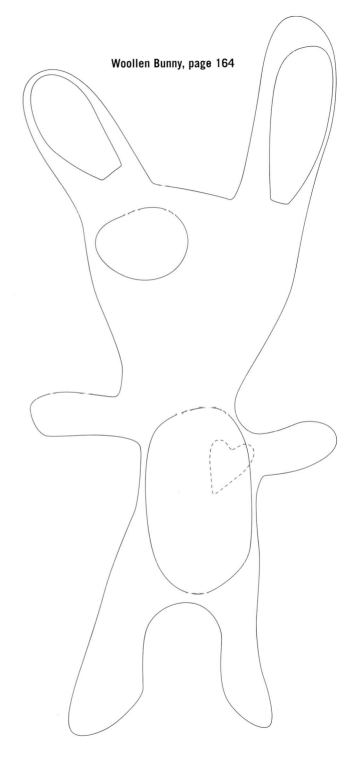

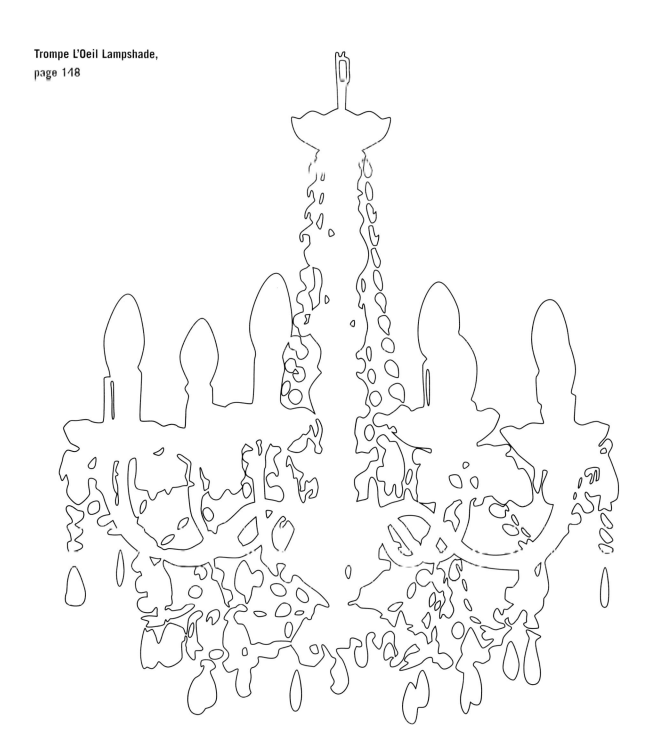

Trompe L'Oeil Lampshade,
page 148

Rainy Day Skirt, page 88

index

resources

Celestial
162 Archway Road
London
N6 5BB
Tel: 0208 341 2788
Retailers of designer buttons and
trimmings

Dyeshop UK
Tel: 0800 170 1107
Web site: www.dyeshop.co.uk
Specialist online supplier of a wide
range of fabric dyes

Fabric UK
Tel: 0800 170 1107
Web site: www.fabricuk.com
Specialist online supplier of a wide
range of fabrics, fabric dyes and
sewing supplies

Fred Aldous
37 Lever Street
Manchester
M1 1LW
Tel: 0161 236 4224
Web site: www.fabricuk.com
Retailer of sewing and craft supplies

Hobbycraft
Tel: 0800 027 2387 for your nearest
branch
Web site: www.hobbycraft.co.uk
Art and craft superstores

John Lewis (Head Office)
Partnership House
Carlisle Place
London
SW1 1BX
Tel: 08456 049 049
Web site: www.JohnLewis.com
Fabrics, trimmings, general sewing and
hobby supplies

Liberty Plc
Regent Street
London
W1B 5AH
Tel: 0207 734 1234
Web site: www.liberty.co.uk
Fabrics, trimmings, general sewing
supplies

Sew Essential
Tel: 01922 722276
Web site: www.sewessential.co.uk
Specialist online supplier of quiting and
patchwork supplies, freezer paper,
crochet supplies, fabric and
haberdashery

Simply Sequins
Tel: 023 9232 5882
Web site: www.simplysequins.co.uk
Specialist online supplier of sequins,
beads and buttons

Texere Yarns
College Mill
Barkerend Road
Bradford
BD1 4AU
Tel: 01274 722191
Web site: www.texere.co.uk
Supplier of embroidery yarns and
feltmaking supplies

VV Rouleaux
54 Sloane Square
Cliveden Place
London
SW1 8AW
Tel: 0207 730 3125
Web site: www.vvrouleaux.com
Supplier of ribbons, trimmings, tassels,
tie-backs and silk flowers

acknowledgements

I would like to thank so many people for making my first book possible.

My wonderful editors, Michelle, Katie and Marie for taking a chance on this first-time author, letting me be myself at all times and showing me a great time in London! My agent, Lauren, for keeping me organised and sane. I'm not sure how I could have done this without you and honestly, I'd rather not think about it.

An amazing creative team: Michael and Mark for making the projects come alive with wonderful photography; Gemma for creative vision; Ella for 'getting my aesthetic' and making the models look fierce! Christina for recommending me to Michelle – without you, this book wouldn't exist! Anne for helping me 'make the pretty'; and Kim for her skilled hands and crochet expertise. All the Department of Craft folks for being crafty gods and goddesses. My crafty gal-pals near and far: Courtney, Daisy, Jenn C, Jenn S, Kari, Linda, Lorelei, Margaret, Meredith, Sarah G, Sarah O'C, Sherri, Susan and all the other glitter girls and crafty bloggers out there. I couldn't imagine better friends and inspirations.

My family, especially my four parents, Patty and Steve and Michael and Tricia and my little brother, Jesse, for always being supportive and never questioning why I would want to play with fabric for a living. A big extra thanks to my mum, Patty, who spent one crazy fall weekend helping me make things and who has been my crafty super-hero since day one. And one giant thanks to Adam, my partner in life and craft. Thank you for your encouragement, love and patience. You are amazing.

Love crafts?

Crafters...keep updated on all exciting craft news from Collins & Brown.
Email lovecrafts@anovabooks.com to register for free email alerts on
forthcoming titles and author events.